Big League Trivia

Facts, Figures, Oddities, and Coincidences

from our National Pastime

Madison McEntire

Bloomington, IN Milton Keynes, UK

authorHOUSE™

AuthorHouse™
1663 Liberty Drive, Suite 200
Bloomington, IN 47403
www.authorhouse.com
Phone: 1-800-839-8640

AuthorHouse™ UK Ltd.
500 Avebury Boulevard
Central Milton Keynes, MK9 2BE
www.authorhouse.co.uk
Phone: 08001974150

First published by AuthorHouse 2/16/2006

ISBN: 1-4259-1292-3 (sc)

Library of Congress Control Number: 2006900045

Printed in the United States of America
Bloomington, Indiana

This book is printed on acid-free paper.

To my wife, Crissy. Thanks for all your love and support, for being patient with me as I spent a lot of time putting this book together, and for at least pretending to be interested when I begin rattling off new baseball trivia items that have come to my attention.

To my children, Mackenzie (age 9) and Will (age 5 1/2). Nothing brings me more joy than spending time with you. Someday too soon, I will miss playing ball with you in the yard and coaching your teams. I am proud of you, love you both dearly – and promise that the Cubs will win a World Series in your lifetime.

"Correct thinkers think that "baseball trivia"
is an oxymoron: Nothing about baseball is trivial."

-- George Will in his column of April 8, 1990

Contents

Introduction

I can't remember not loving the game of baseball – there's a book on my shelf at home called *The Greatest in Baseball* that I bought in the third grade. Although the small Arkansas town where I grew up dropped their baseball program when I was around ten years old, my love of the game grew as I got older. Some of the credit goes to my grandmother, Brooxie Karns, who bought me baseball books each year for Christmas and my birthday, always signing inside the cover – and still does to this day. They are some of my most prized possessions. Another big moment was in August 1983 when we got cable TV, finally allowing me to watch a ballgame almost every day. I immediately fell in love with the Cubs and Harry Caray, only to have my heart broken a year later by the 1984 Cubs – still my favorite team ever. At the University of Arkansas in the fall of 1989, I met Crissy who, naturally, knew nothing about baseball. So later in October after the Cubs lost the 1989 NLCS, it was funny, but sad, when she attempted to cheer me up by actually saying, "Don't worry, there's always next year." In June 2000, I found out exactly how much she loves me when she patiently, and without complaining, sat through over five hours of rain delays while seven months pregnant just so I could see Mark McGwire's 550th career home run become official. I love to visit ballparks each summer and have been fortunate enough to see games in 23 different major league parks, including a ten-game bus tour along the East Coast in July 1998 with my father and another seven-game tour through the Midwest with Dad and Will in August 2005.

The game of baseball appeals to me in many different ways – it has a rich, wonderful history and a lot of managerial strategy to dissect – but the one area that has always fascinated me the most is the vast amount of numbers and trivia that baseball produces with its day-to-day schedule. In any given game, something could happen that has rarely, if ever, happened before. I've always had the gift (or is it a curse?) of retaining a large amount of the facts, numbers, and stories that I have read, seen, or heard over the years. Every couple weeks or so, Crissy will ask me some form of the question, "How can you remember Babe Ruth's lifetime batting average but can't remember which shirt goes with that pair of pants?" I just smile and tell her that I only remember the important things!

I never set out with the specific intention of writing this book – it came about as a result of my love of baseball and love of reading. This work literally began well over ten years ago when I began jotting down a few things that I found interesting while looking through *Total Baseball* or one of the other baseball reference books in my study. Over the years, I added to the list off-and-on as I researched interesting items that I read, saw on TV, or discovered on my own, until one day it dawned on me that I had enough material to think about doing a book. There are a few other things you should know before beginning. Rather than a simple question-and-answer format like many baseball trivia books, I decided upon a paragraph format, which allows for much more detail – probably much more than you want in many cases. Unless stated otherwise, I used the year 1900 – the beginning of the modern baseball era – as the starting point for the items in this book. I also chose not to use the word "postseason". Not only is it possibly the most overused word in all of sports, it is inaccurate to me since every team makes "the postseason". Most teams – like my Cubs – just spend it at home. "Playoffs" is a more exciting word and also helps keep the World Series and its great history separate from the League Championship Series and the League Division Series. Finally, new ballparks of the last several years have opened with a corporate name intact, so there is really no other way to refer to them. For the older parks from my youth, I decided to call them by the name they had then, so in this book it is Candlestick Park, Riverfront Stadium, etc. – no matter when their naming rights were sold to the highest bidder.

I used many resources for the contents of this book. My membership in the Society for American Baseball Research (SABR) was a huge advantage. The SABR publications alone are worth the price of membership (see www.sabr.org), but being a SABR member also includes access to ProQuest Historical Newspapers, which allowed me to use the digital archives of *The New York Times*, *Washington Post*, and *Los Angeles Times*. Another important source was the fabulous Retrosheet website which provided lots of play-by-play game accounts, box scores, and transaction information. Finally, the incredible Sabermetric Baseball Encyclopedia by Lee Sinins (available at www.baseball-encyclopedia.com) was an invaluable tool for sorting stats and checking data. Thanks to David Vincent, who maintains the SABR home run database, for answering an occasional home run question and to Dave Smith and the other fine people at Retrosheet for all the free information available at www.retrosheet. org. Many other SABR members answered a particular question, provided information that I requested, or, perhaps unknowingly, gave me an idea for an item in this book. I am sure that I am leaving someone out, but I want to thank Scott Flatow, Bill Nowlin, Bob Bogart, Bill Deane, John Skipper, Steve Gietschier, Dave Zeman, and Fred Worth. Thanks to Chris Reynolds for providing my photo for this book. Special thanks to Terry Turner – I enjoy our baseball trivia lunches at Jimmy's Serious Sandwiches. We never seem to run out of interesting baseball topics to discuss.

----- Madison McEntire

All-Star Game

The National League managed only three hits in the 1995 All-Star Game and still won – *because all three hits were home runs.* They beat the American League 3-2 at The Ballpark in Arlington, although Frank Thomas put the AL on the scoreboard first when he drove in both American League runs with a two-run homer in the fourth. After being held hitless for 5.2 innings, the NL finally got untracked when Craig Biggio homered against Dennis Martinez. Mike Piazza followed with a homer in the seventh off hometown favorite Kenny Rogers and Jeff Conine hit the game-winner against Steve Ontiveros in the eighth. The NL finished the game with no runners left on base because their only other batter to reach was Lenny Dykstra who led off the game with a walk and was caught stealing.

Mickey Owen is the only player to homer in the All-Star Game in a season in which he did not hit a regular season home run. Owen batted 421 times for the Dodgers in the 1942 regular season without belting a single long ball. In the All-Star Game at the Polo Grounds on July 6, Owen pinch-hit for pitcher Claude Passeau in the eighth inning and homered into the left field stands against Detroit's Al Benton, accounting for the National League's lone run in their 3-1 loss.

The National League is *undefeated* in the ten extra-inning All-Star Games. The NL won in 1950 (14 innings), 1955 (12 innings), the first All-Star Game of the 1961 season (ten innings), 1966 (ten innings), 1967 (15 innings), 1970 (12 innings), 1972 (ten innings),

1987 (13 innings), and 1994 (ten innings). The 2002 All-Star Game was declared a 7-7 tie after 11 innings because each side ran out of pitchers. However, the NL has never scored more than nine runs in an All-Star Game. The double-digit mark has been reached six times in All-Star competition by the American League. They did it in 1946, 1949, 1954, 1983, 1992, and 1998.

The All-Star Game MVP award was first handed out in 1962, and through the 1996 game no player from the host team claimed the trophy – *but then happened twice in three years.* In the 1997 Midsummer Classic, Sandy Alomar, Jr. clouted a two-run homer in the seventh inning that provided the margin of victory for the American League as they beat the National League 3-1 at Cleveland's Jacobs Field. Two years later at Fenway Park, Boston's Pedro Martinez struck out five in just two innings and was the winning pitcher as the AL triumphed 4-1. Martinez struck out Barry Larkin, Larry Walker and Sammy Sosa in order in the first and then fanned Mark McGwire to start the second. After Matt Williams reached on an error by second baseman Roberto Alomar, Martinez fanned Jeff Bagwell with Williams being thrown out attempting to steal second base.

Rick Dempsey played in 1,766 games over 24 seasons (1969-1992) but was never selected to an All-Star team.

Terry Steinbach is the only player to hit a home run in both his first major league at-bat and his first All-Star at-bat. Steinbach made his debut for Oakland at Municipal Stadium in Cleveland on September 12, 1986, by replacing starting catcher Mickey Tettleton in the sixth inning and then led off the seventh with a homer against Cleveland's Greg Swindell. In the 1988 season, despite hitting just .217 with 19 RBIs in 46 games before the All-Star break, Steinbach was chosen as the American League starting catcher (from a weak group of AL catchers) due to questionable balloting practices by the Oakland fans. He immediately justified his selection when he led of the third at Riverfront Stadium and swatted Dwight Gooden's second pitch to right field, where it went off the glove of a leaping Darryl Strawberry and over the fence for a home run to give the AL a 1-0 lead. It was the AL's first All-Star run since the seventh inning of the 1986 game, ending the NL's shutout streak at 17 innings. In the fourth inning Steinbach just missed a grand slam against Bob Knepper, settling for a long sacrifice fly to give the AL a 2-0 advantage. The AL held on to win 2-1, and Steinbach was named the game's MVP.

Fred Lynn is the only player to hit a grand slam in an All-Star Game. In the 1983 contest at Comiskey Park, Lynn hammered a third-inning pitch from Atlee Hammaker into the lower right field stands to give the American League a 9-1 lead. The blast accounted for the last four of the All-Star record seven runs allowed by Hammaker – *with all seven scoring in the third inning*. The American League went on to win 13-3, ending the National League's All-Star Game winning streak at 11 games.

Despite winning MVP awards in 1982 and 1989 and compiling career totals of 3,142 hits, 251 homers and 1,406 RBIs in his 20-year career, Hall of Fame shortstop Robin Yount played in just three All-Star Games (1980, 1982, and 1983). He was 0-7 with a sacrifice fly.

From 1995 to 2000, Dodgers' first baseman Eric Karros had five seasons of more than 30 homers and 100 RBIs – *but was never chosen to an All-Star team*. During this six-year period, the National League was represented at first base twice each by Fred McGriff, Jeff Bagwell, Mark Grace, Mark McGwire, and Andres Galarraga, and one time each by Sean Casey and Todd Helton.

Joe DiMaggio is the only player to get hits during an All-Star Game at each of the three classic New York ballparks. DiMaggio homered at Yankee Stadium in the 1939 All-Star Game and collected two hits in both the 1942 game at the Polo Grounds and the 1949 game at Ebbets Field. He also had one All-Star hit at Briggs Stadium (later renamed Tiger Stadium) in 1941 and at Wrigley Field in 1947. DiMaggio did not appear at the 1946 All-Star Game played at Fenway Park.

Washington's Dean Stone was the winning pitcher of the 1954 All-Star Game played at Cleveland's Municipal Stadium – *despite not retiring a batter.* Stone entered the game with the American League trailing 9-8 with two outs in the eighth inning and runners on the corners. With Duke Snider at the plate, Red Schoendienst attempted to steal home but was tagged out by catcher Yogi Berra to end the inning. In the bottom of the inning, Larry Doby pinch-hit for Stone and tied the game with a one-out home run to left-center field. Following singles by Berra and Mickey Mantle and a walk to Al Rosen, Nellie Fox blooped a single over second base to give the AL an 11-9 lead and make Stone the pitcher of record. Virgil Trucks came on in the ninth and held the NL scoreless to secure Stone's victory.

The 1934 All-Star Game at New York's Polo Grounds is best known for the performance by New York's Carl Hubbell who, after giving up a lead-off single and a walk to begin the game, struck out five consecutive Hall of Famers. Hubbell whiffed Babe Ruth, Lou Gehrig and Jimmie Foxx to end the first, and then he struck out Al Simmons and Joe Cronin to begin the second. Bill Dickey, another Hall of Famer, ended the streak with a single before Hubbell struck out yet another member of the Hall of Fame, pitcher Lefty Gomez, to end the frame. The 1934 game also featured the only steal of home in All-Star play. Pittsburgh's Pie Traynor swiped home as part of a double steal with Mel Ott in the fifth inning. Traynor's steal got the NL to within a run at 8-7, but the AL went on to win 9-7.

Dodgers' closer Eric Gagne was perfect in 55 save opportunities in the 2003 regular season – *but blew the save in the 2003 All-Star game.* With the National League clinging to a 6-4 lead at Comiskey Park, Gagne gave up a one-out double to Garret Anderson. Following a ground out, Vernon Wells doubled and the American League took a 7-6 lead on a two-run, pinch-hit homer by Hank Blalock. Gagne's 2003 season was part of his record 84 consecutive successful save opportunities, a streak that ended on July 5, 2004, when he could not hold a 5-3 lead against the Diamondbacks. His previous blown save had also come against the Diamondbacks on August 22, 2002.

Award Winners

Four players have won MVP awards with two teams, and four players have won the award at different positions – but Alex Rodriguez is the only one to do *both*. Rodriguez won his first MVP as the Rangers' shortstop in 2003 when he hit .298 with 47 homers and 118 RBIs. Two years later he played third base for the Yankees and won MVP honors with 48 homers, 130 RBIs and a .321 batting average.

Sandy Alomar, Jr. is the only player to win the Rookie of the Year Award after beginning his career in the other league. In 1988 and 1989, Alomar appeared in a total of eight games for the San Diego Padres and got four hits in 20 at-bats, including a three-run home run against San Francisco's Rick Reuschel on September 30, 1989. Alomar was included in a trade with Cleveland in December that brought Joe Carter to San Diego and then hit .290 with nine homers and 66 RBIs for the Indians in 1990 to win the AL Rookie of the Year award.

From 1970 to 1977, Cincinnati Reds' players dominated the National League MVP Award, winning it six times in eight years. Johnny Bench won in 1970 and 1972, followed by Pete Rose in 1973, Joe Morgan in 1975 and 1976, and George Foster in 1977. The Reds have had just one MVP since – Barry Larkin in 1995.

Frank Robinson is the only player to win the MVP award in each league. In 1961 with the Cincinnati Reds, Robinson was voted

National League MVP for hitting .323 with 37 home runs, 124 RBIs, and 117 runs scored. After being traded to the Baltimore Orioles following the 1965 season, Robinson responded with another MVP season by winning the 1966 American League Triple Crown with a .316 average, 49 home runs and 122 RBIs and also leading the AL with 122 runs scored. Robinson's Triple Crown season was the *only time* he led the league in home runs, RBIs, or batting average. His 1966 batting championship is also the only time an Oriole batter has led the league in hitting.

In the history of the MVP Award there has been only one tie. Willie Stargell and Keith Hernandez each got 216 of 336 possible points for the 1979 NL MVP Award. Stargell belted 32 home runs, knocked in 82 runs, and batted .281 while leading the Pittsburgh Pirates to the National League pennant. Hernandez led the NL with a .344 average, 116 runs scored, and 48 doubles to go with 105 RBIs for the St. Louis Cardinals. In the voting by the Baseball Writers Association, Stargell received ten first-place votes – to just four for Hernandez – but also received two sixth-place votes. Hernandez made up the difference by getting more second, third, fourth, and fifth-place votes than Stargell.

Boston Red Sox great Ted Williams won the Triple Crown twice – but was not voted the American League MVP *either time*. Williams hit .356 and topped the AL in 1942 with 36 home runs and 137 RBIs and still finished second in the MVP balloting to the New York Yankees' Joe Gordon who batted .322 with 18 home runs and 103 RBIs. In 1947 Williams posted AL bests with a .343 average, 32 homers and 114 RBIs but again finished second, one vote behind Joe DiMaggio (.315, 20 home runs, 97 RBIs).

Detroit's Hal Newhouser is the only pitcher to win back-to-back MVP awards. Newhouser won in 1944 by compiling a record of 29-9 with a 2.22 ERA and took the trophy again the following season by going 25-9 with a 1.81 ERA and 212 strikeouts in 1945.

In 1987 Kevin Seitzer had an outstanding rookie season for the Kansas City Royals. Seitzer appeared in 161 games and hit .323

with 207 hits, 15 homers, 83 RBIs, and 105 runs scored – and still finished second in the Rookie of the Year balloting. He had the misfortune of being in the same rookie class with Mark McGwire who hit 49 homers – still the major league record for a rookie – and drove in 118 runs.

The Los Angeles Dodgers had four consecutive Rookie of the Year Award winners from 1979 to 1982 (Rick Sutcliffe, Steve Howe, Fernando Valenzuela, and Steve Sax) and another five straight winners from 1992 to 1996 (Eric Karros, Mike Piazza, Raul Mondesi, Hideo Nomo, and Todd Hollandsworth). The Oakland A's, with Rookie of the Year Award winners from 1986 to 1988 (Jose Canseco, Mark McGwire, and Walt Weiss), are the only other team to have three consecutive winners.

From 1956 to 1966, when the Cy Young Award was given to only one pitcher in baseball rather than one in each league, Los Angles Dodger great Sandy Koufax won three times – and the voting was *unanimous* each time. Koufax led all major league pitchers in 1963 with 306 strikeouts and an ERA of 1.88 and tied Juan Marichal for the most wins with 25. In 1965 Koufax won his second Cy Young when he posted major league-leading totals of 26 wins, 382 strikeouts, and a 2.04 ERA. The 1966 season proved to be Koufax's last due to an arthritic elbow condition, but he finished in style by leading all pitchers with 27 wins, 317 strikeouts and a 1.73 ERA. Despite never having an ERA under 3.00 in his first seven seasons, Koufax posted earned run averages of 2.54, 1.88, 1.74, 2.04, and 1.73 from 1962 to 1966.

Lou Gehrig won the 1934 American League Triple Crown with an average of .363, 49 homers, and 165 RBIs – and still finished *fifth* in the American League MVP voting. Mickey Cochrane led Detroit to a pennant-winning 101 wins and was voted MVP, despite hitting just two homers and driving in only 76 RBIs to go with his .320 average. Charlie Gehringer, another Tiger, finished with a .356 average, 11 homers, and 127 RBIs and was second in the voting. Yankees' pitcher Lefty Gomez was 26-5 with a 2.33 ERA and ended up in third place, just ahead of Tiger hurler Schoolboy Rowe (24-8, 3.45 ERA) who finished fourth.

Butch Metzger won just 18 games in his career but tied for the 1976 National League Rookie of the Year Award with Cincinnati's Pat Zachry. After one victory in both 1974 and 1975, in a total of just 18 innings, Metzger was 11-4 with 16 saves and a 2.92 ERA in 77 relief appearances for the San Diego Padres. He would pitch in another 100 games but win just five more times before his career ended in 1978.

Randy Jones is the only starting pitcher to win the Cy Young Award while striking out fewer than 100 batters. Jones was 22-14 with a 2.74 ERA for the 1976 San Diego Padres, leading the National League with 25 complete games and 315.1 innings pitched, but he struck out only 93 hitters.

Derek Jeter is the only player to be named MVP in both the All-Star Game and the World Series in the same season. At the 2000 All-Star Game in Atlanta, Jeter led the American League to 6-3 victory by going 3 for 3 with a double, two RBIs, and a run scored. His performance made him the first Yankee to win the All-Star MVP award. That fall in the World Series, Jeter propelled the Yankees to a five-game win over the New York Mets, hitting .409 (9 for 22) with two doubles, a triple, and two homers while scoring six runs. The only other player to win both awards *at any time* in his career is Frank Robinson, who was the World Series MVP in 1966 and the All-Star Game MVP in 1971.

Although made up of only four teams, the American League West produced the AL MVP for *nine consecutive seasons*. From 1996 to 2004, the AL MVPs were Juan Gonzalez (Texas, 1996 and 1998), Ken Griffey, Jr. (Seattle, 1997), Ivan Rodriguez (Texas, 1999), Jason Giambi (Oakland, 2000), Ichiro Suzuki (Seattle, 2001), Miguel Tejada (Oakland, 2002), Alex Rodriguez (Texas, 2003) and Vladimir Guerrero (Anaheim, 2004). Despite the nine MVPs, just one AL West team made a World Series appearance during that span – the 2002 Anaheim Angels who beat San Francisco in seven games.

Fred Lynn and Ichiro Suzuki are the only players to win the Rookie of the Year Award and be named MVP in the same season. Lynn did it with the Red Sox in 1975 when he hit .331 with 21 home runs and 105 RBIs. He also led the AL with 47 doubles and 103 runs scored. Suzuki won with Seattle in 2001 when he paced the AL with a .350 average, 242 hits and 56 steals.

Willie Stargell is the only player to win the regular season MVP award and be named MVP of both the LCS and World Series all in the same season. In 1979 Stargell tied with Keith Hernandez for NL MVP when he hit 32 homers and had 82 RBIs. In the Pirates' three-game sweep of Cincinnati in the NLCS, he was 5 for 11 with a double, two homers and six RBIs. Stargell then led the Pirates to a seven-game World Series triumph over the Baltimore Orioles by going 12 for 30 at the plate with four doubles, all three Pirate homers, seven RBIs, and seven runs scored.

Pittsburgh beat New York in seven games in the 1960 World Series, but Yankees' second baseman Bobby Richardson was voted the World Series MVP – making him the only player from the *losing* team to win the award. Coming off a regular season in which he collected just 12 doubles, three triples, one home run, and 26 RBIs in 460 at-bats, Richardson batted .367 with two doubles, two triples, one homer, and 12 RBIs in the 1960 Series.

Lou Piniella is the only player to win the Rookie of the Year Award while playing with his third club. At the age of 21, Piniella batted one time in four games with Baltimore in September 1964, but his next major league action was not until September 1968 when he batted five times in six games with Cleveland. Piniella was selected by the Seattle Pilots in the 1968 expansion draft but before playing for them was traded to Kansas City where he hit .282 with 11 homers and 68 RBIs to win American League Rookie of the Year honors in 1969.

Don Newcombe is the only pitcher to be named the Rookie of the Year and win both the MVP and Cy Young Awards. Newcombe was the NL's top rookie in 1949 when he was 17-8 with 149 strikeouts and a 3.17 ERA. He won the first Cy Young Award and the NL MVP in 1956 when he was 27-7 with a 3.06 ERA.

The 1968 season is the only season in which pitchers won the MVP Award in each league. Bob Gibson dominated the National League, finishing with a record of 22-9, 268 strikeouts and a microscopic 1.12 ERA for the Cardinals. Eight of Gibson's losses were by either one or two runs, including two games by the score of 1-0 and three others by a 3-2 score. The American League winner was Denny McLain who went 31-6 with 280 strikeouts and a 1.96 ERA and became the first 30-game winner since Dizzy Dean in 1934. Since 1968 the NL has not had another pitcher win the MVP award, but five AL hurlers have done so – Vida Blue (1971), Rollie Fingers (1981), Willie Hernandez (1984), Roger Clemens (1986) and Dennis Eckersley (1992).

On September 7, 1996, rookie Scott Rolen's season ended when he was hit by a pitch from Cubs' pitcher Steve Trachsel and suffered a broken arm. Rolen finished the season with 130 at-bats – the *maximum* allowable for him to still qualify as a rookie for the following season. Rolen came back the next season to hit .283 with 21 homers and 92 RBIs for the Phillies, and he was unanimously voted the 1997 National League Rookie of the Year.

Rick Sutcliffe won the NL Cy Young Award in 1984 – *despite beginning the year in the American League.* Sutcliffe was 4-5 with a 5.15 ERA in 15 games for the Cleveland Indians when he was traded to the Chicago Cubs in a seven-player trade on June 13. He won his first two games for Chicago but was then rocked for eight hits and five earned runs in just four innings on June 29 at Los Angeles. From that point, Sutcliffe went 14-0 in his last 17 starts to finish 16-1 with a 2.69 ERA in the NL and lead the Cubs to the division title.

Ballparks

Pittsburgh Pirate slugger Willie Stargell hit a home run in the first game played at three ballparks. The New York Mets opened Shea Stadium on April 17, 1964, but Stargell stole the show and led the Pirates to a 4-3 win. In his first at-bat, Stargell hit the park's first homer against Jack Fisher in the second inning. He later added a double and two singles and also scored the winning run in the top of the ninth on a single by Bill Mazeroski. In the inaugural game at Atlanta's Fulton County Stadium on April 12, 1966, Stargell hammered a two-run homer in the 13th inning against Tony Cloninger to lead the Pirates to a 3-2 win. The Pirates moved from Forbes Field to Three Rivers Stadium on July 16, 1970, and Stargell smashed the Pirates' first homer when he connected for a sixth-inning shot against Gary Nolan in Pittsburgh's 3-2 loss to the Reds.

The first four games played in Oriole Park at Camden Yards were shutouts. Baltimore won the inaugural game on April 6, 1992, by blanking the Cleveland Indians 2-0. The Indians rebounded two days later to win 4-0 but then were blanked 2-0 by the Orioles the next day. Following their first road trip of the year, Baltimore returned home on April 17 and beat the Detroit Tigers 8-0.

Cleveland's Jacobs Field opened for the beginning of the 1994 season, but no batter hit an inside-the-park home run until David Bell did it on April 15, 1998 – in his *first* plate appearance with the Indians. Just acquired off waivers from St. Louis, Bell stepped to the plate in the first inning and slapped a pitch from Randy Johnson high off the left field wall, circled the bases, and slid home safely as the Mariners' infield mishandled the relay throw.

The biggest shutout in the history of Chicago's new Comiskey Park occurred in the park's *very first game*. The White Sox opened their new home on April 18, 1991, by getting pounded 16-0 by the Detroit Tigers. Cecil Fielder started the barrage by hitting the first home run in the new park, a three-run blast run against Jack McDowell in the third, and the Tigers put the game out of reach by scoring ten runs in the fourth. The Tigers knocked out 19 hits, including Fielder's homer, two homers by Rob Deer, and a three-run shot by Tony Phillips. The White Sox were also blanked in the first game played at the original Comiskey Park when the St. Louis Browns beat them 2-0 on July 1, 1910.

Juan Gonzalez hit the first home run at Detroit's Comerica Park on April 14, 2000, when he blasted a three-run shot against Tampa Bay's Ryan Rupe in the third inning of the fourth game played at the new park. Later in the season on September 2, Gonzalez also hit the first inside-the-park homer at Comerica. Facing his old team, the Texas Rangers, he hit a pitch from Kenny Rogers off the top of the center field wall. The ball caromed off the leg of Rangers' center fielder Gabe Kapler – who was involved in the trade that brought Gonzalez to Detroit – and rolled along the wall toward right field. Gonzalez circled the bases and scored standing up, easily beating the off-line relay throw.

Michael Tucker hit the first home run at two ballparks. Tucker blasted the first homer at Atlanta's Turner Field when he connected off Chicago's Kevin Foster in the third inning on April 4, 1997. Four years later with Cincinnati on April 6, 2001, he homered against Brewers' hurler Jeff D'Amico in the fourth to become the first player to go deep at Milwaukee's Miller Park. Tucker also got the last hit at Milwaukee's County Stadium on September 28, 2000, getting an eighth-inning infield single against Juan Acevedo, and he hit the first double at Pittsburgh's PNC Park when he faced Todd Ritchie on April 9, 2001.

Frank Tanana spoiled the festivities at three different ballparks with complete-game victories. Tanana and the Angles won the first game at the Kingdome in Seattle on April 6, 1977, when he scattered nine hits, fanned nine, and blanked the Mariners 7-0. On April 18, 1991, Tanana, now with Detroit, allowed seven hits and went the distance during the inaugural game at Chicago's new Comiskey Park as the Tigers pounded the White Sox 16-0. During the eighth inning, Tanana even batted for the first time in his 18-year career and struck out on three pitches. At the end of the season on October 6, 1991, Tanana allowed only four hits as the Tigers beat the Orioles 7-1 in the last game at Baltimore's Memorial Stadium.

Yankee Stadium is known as "The House that Ruth Built" and, fittingly enough, Babe Ruth hit the first Yankee Stadium home run in the park's inaugural game on April 18, 1923. With New York up 1-0 in the third inning, Ruth belted a three-run homer against Howard Ehmke and led the Yankees to a 4-1 win over his former team, the Boston Red Sox.

The Cincinnati Reds were the visiting team in the first game at six ballparks. They played the inaugural game at Forbes Field (April 22, 1909), Dodger Stadium (April 10, 1962), Three Rivers Stadium (July 16, 1970), Miller Park (April 6, 2001), PNC Park (April 9, 2001), and Citizens Bank Park (April 12, 2004). The Reds also played in the first National League game at Weeghman Park (renamed Wrigley Field in 1926) on April 20, 1916, after the park had served as the home of the Chicago Federal League team for the previous two years. The Reds also closed down Milwaukee's County Stadium with a win on September 28, 2000, and lost the last regular season game at Busch Stadium in St. Louis on October 2, 2005. In addition to meeting the Pirates in the first game at Forbes Field and PNC Park, the Reds played also them in the first game at Cincinnati's new Great American Ballpark on March 31, 2003.

Jimmy Rollins' first two career inside-the-park home runs were also the first ones hit at each of the new ballparks that opened in 2004 – Philadelphia's Citizens Bank Park and San Diego's Petco Park. In his home ballpark in Philadelphia on June 20, Rollins hammered a second-inning pitch from Kansas City's Dennys Reyes to center field where Royals' outfielder Carlos Beltran went back and attempted a leaping catch but missed the ball. Rollins' drive ricocheted off the wall and bounded back toward center field, allowing the speedy Phillie shortstop to circle the bases for a three-run homer. At Petco Park on August 4, Rollins scored without a throw to the plate when he lined a fourth-inning pitch from Adam Eaton that hit near the base of the foul pole in right field and caromed into the Phillies' bullpen in foul ground. Padre right fielder Brain Giles, who had been playing Rollins toward center field, had a long run to the ball and then had trouble picking it up because it had rolled under a bullpen bench that was littered with cups and other trash.

The National League's Philadelphia Phillies abandoned the Baker Bowl on July 4, 1938, and began playing their home games in Shibe Park, the home of their American League crosstown rivals, the Philadelphia A's. At the time of the Phillies' move to Shibe, Hall of Famer Mel Ott had 325 career homers for the New York Giants. Over the next 7 1/2 years, Ott would hit 189 more homers but hit just .220 (59 for 268) in 71 games at Shibe Park, never homering against the Phillies in their ballpark.

Sean Casey collected the first hit at both Miller Park and PNC Park. On April 6, 2001, at Milwaukee's new Miller Park, Casey singled to center field against Jeff D'Amico to lead off the top of the second inning and three days later christened PNC Park with a first-inning homer against Pirate hurler Todd Ritchie. Casey also hit the last home run at Milwaukee's County Stadium, a three-run shot in the fifth inning against D'Amico on September 28, 2000.

Cincinnati's Riverfront Stadium was the site where Hank Aaron tied Babe Ruth's home record on April 4, 1974, with a three-run homer against Reds' pitcher Jack Billingham and where Pete Rose broke Ty Cobb's hit record on September 11, 1985, when he singled off San Diego pitcher Eric Show. Aaron not only tied Babe Ruth's home run record at Riverfront Stadium, he hit the park's first home run on June 30, 1970.

Paul Sorrento singled against Rick Sutcliffe for the first hit at Baltimore's Camden Yards on April 6, 1992, and hit the park's first home run when he blasted a three-run homer against Bob Milacki in the first inning of its second game on April 8. On May 9, 1995, Sorrento hit a grand slam against Kansas City's Doug Linton – the first slam hit at Cleveland's Jacobs Field.

Greg Maddux was the winning pitcher in the last game at both Mile High Stadium and Veterans Stadium. On August 11, 1994, Maddux went the distance, allowing just three hits and striking out four, and beat the Rockies 13-0. The baseball strike of 1994 began the following day and eventually ended the season – and Colorado's two-year stay at Mile High because they moved into Coors Field for the 1995 season. After 33 seasons in Veterans Stadium, the Phillies closed down the park with a 5-2 loss to the Braves on September 28, 2003. Maddux gave up two runs on four hits to get the win despite pitching just five innings.

Coincidences

Frank Thomas and Jeff Bagwell share the same birthday (May 27, 1968) and each won an MVP award as a first baseman in 1994. Thomas won the American League MVP with the Chicago White Sox by hitting .353 with 38 home runs, 101 RBIs and a league-leading 106 runs scored. Bagwell captured the National League MVP with the Houston Astros as he averaged .368 with 39 homers and led the NL with 116 RBIs and 104 runs. As late as August 6, 2004, they were tied with 436 career home runs each. Entering the 2006 season, Bagwell holds a one-homer lead over Thomas (449 to 448). The duo almost made their first World Series appearances together. In the White Sox's four-game sweep of the Astros in 2005, Bagwell had one hit in eight at-bats, but Thomas suffered a season-ending ankle injury in July that prevented him from playing.

Cesar Geronimo was the 3,000th strikeout victim of both Bob Gibson and Nolan Ryan. On July 17, 1974, Gibson fanned Geronimo in the second inning at Busch Stadium to become the only pitcher other than Walter Johnson to register 3,000 strikeouts. Ryan became the fourth pitcher with 3,000 Ks when he struck Geronimo out to lead off the second inning on July 4, 1980, at Riverfront Stadium.

Braves' pitcher Pat Jarvis was the first of Nolan Ryan's 5,714 strikeout victims and the hurler who gave up Ernie Banks' 500th home run. Ryan whiffed Jarvis, the first batter he faced, when he made his big league debut for the New York Mets in the sixth inning on September 11, 1966. Banks hit his milestone homer against Jarvis in the bottom of the second on May 12, 1970, at Wrigley Field in a game that the Braves eventually lost 4-3 in 11 innings.

Steve Garvey was playing first base for the Los Angeles Dodgers when Hank Aaron broke Babe Ruth's record for career home runs on April 8, 1974, and was playing first base for the San Diego Padres when Pete Rose broke Ty Cobb's hit record on September 11, 1985. He was the only player to appear in both games.

Hall of Fame outfielder Dave Winfield was born on October 3, 1951 – the day Bobby Thomson hit his famous home run against Brooklyn Dodger Ralph Branca to win the NL pennant for the New York Giants.

Although there have been only 13 players win the Triple Crown since 1900, the city of Philadelphia boasted two winners in 1933. Phillies' slugger Chuck Klein led the National League with a .368 average, 28 home runs and 120 RBIs. Meanwhile, Philadelphia A's star Jimmie Foxx's .356 average, 48 homers, and 163 RBIs topped the American League.

On September 29, 1963, St. Louis Cardinals' great Stan Musial wrapped up his distinguished career against the Cincinnati Reds at Sportsman's Park in St. Louis. He slapped out two singles to push his National League record for hits to 3,630 – and give him 1,815 hits at home and 1,815 hits on the road. Musial entered the game needing to score one run to even the career totals of his RBIs and runs as well. However, his second hit – a single in the sixth – drove in Curt Flood, and then Musial left for a pinch runner, ending his career with 1,951 RBIs and 1,949 runs scored. Playing second base that day for the Reds was rookie Pete Rose (who was 3 for 6 with a double) – the player who would eventually break Musial's NL hit record on August 10, 1981.

Joe Torre hit two home runs, including the first home run, during the first game at Atlanta's Fulton County Stadium on April 12, 1966. Torre connected against Pittsburgh's Bob Veale in the fifth and against Don Schwall in the bottom of the 13th, but it was not enough to overcome Willie Stargell's two-run homer in the top of the inning and the Pirates won 3-2. Braves' hurler Tony Cloninger pitched all 13 innings and was the loser despite giving up just ten hits and striking out 13 Pirates. More than 30 years later as the manager of New York Yankees, Torre led the Yanks to wins against the Braves in Games 3, 4, and 5 of the 1996 World Series – the last three games played in the park.

During his famous 56-game hitting streak from May 15 to July 16 of 1941, Joe DiMaggio banged out 56 singles and scored 56 runs.

On July 23, 1991, Goose Gossage recorded his 308th career save – by preserving Nolan Ryan's *308th* career victory. The Texas Rangers beat the Boston Red Sox 5-4 at Arlington Stadium with Ryan pitching seven innings of three-hit ball, giving up three earned runs and striking out seven. Gossage entered on in the bottom of the eighth to get the last four outs to earn the save – his *only* save of the season.

After 1,727 games in a Los Angeles Dodger uniform from 1969 to 1982, including the last 1,107 consecutively, Steve Garvey joined the San Diego Padres for the 1983 season. On April 15 at Dodger Stadium – in his first game against his former team – Garvey played in his 1,117th consecutive game, tying Billy Williams' National League record. Garvey's consecutive games streak ended at 1,207 games when he dislocated his thumb during a play at the plate against the Braves on July 29.

Diego Segui appeared in the first game for both the Seattle Pilots and the Seattle Mariners. On April 8, 1969, Segui gave up two hits and one earned run in three innings of relief as the Pilots scored four runs in the top of the first inning and then held on to beat the California Angels 4-3. In the Seattle Mariners' inaugural game on April 6, 1977, Segui started against the Angels at the Kingdome and gave up six runs, only four of which were earned, in 3.2 innings and took the loss.

The Florida Marlins beat the same pitcher for both their first regular season win and their first World Series win. On April 5, 1993, the Marlins began play in the National League by beating Orel Hershiser and the Dodgers 6-3. Florida hitters roughed up Hershiser for ten hits and five earned runs, getting three runs in the second on a two-run triple by Walt Weiss and a single by Scott Pose. The victory went to 45-year-old Charlie Hough who pitching six strong innings. After winning the NL Wild Card in 1997, Florida advanced to the World Series against the Cleveland Indians. In Game 1 they hammed Hershiser for seven runs in 4.1 innings, the big blow being a three-run homer by Moises Alou in the fourth, on their way to a 7-4 win.

Ron Guidry was 25-3 for the Yankees in 1978 – *and each loss was to a pitcher named "Mike"*. Guidry, who set a Yankees' record by starting the season with 13 straight wins, suffered his first loss on July 7 at Milwaukee to Mike Caldwell by the score of 6-0. Larry Hisle touched Guidry for two homers, a three-run blast in the first and a solo in the sixth, and Caldwell held the Yankees to just four hits. Guidry's next loss was to Mike Flanagan and Baltimore at Yankee Stadium on August 4. Despite going the distance, giving up just five hits and striking out ten Orioles, Guidry lost 2-1 when Doug DeCinces hit a two-run homer in the seventh. After a string of seven straight wins, Guidry lost his third game of the year to Mike Willis and the Toronto Blue Jays by the score of 8-1 on September 20 at Toronto's Exhibition Stadium. In the first game of a doubleheader, Guidry committed a first-inning throwing error and the Blue Jays capitalized by scoring two unearned runs. In the bottom of the second, Toronto knocked the Yankees' ace from the game by scoring three more times. Guidry's biggest win of the season was also against a pitcher named "Mike". On October 2, Guidry squared off against Mike Torrez at Fenway Park in the famous New York-Boston playoff game to decide the 1978 American League East championship, with Bucky Dent's unlikely home run in the seventh inning against Torrez making a winner out of Guidry.

Hall of Famers Lefty Grove and Ted Lyons are the only pitchers who surrendered one of Babe Ruth's 60 home runs and also gave up a hit to Joe DiMaggio during his 56-game hitting streak. Within a span of nine days at Yankee Stadium in 1927, Ruth hit his 54th homer (a two-run shot) against Lyons on September 18 and his 57th (a grand slam) off Grove on September 27. During his famous hitting streak in 1941, DiMaggio singled against Grove in the 11th game at Yankee Stadium on May 25 and ran the streak to 52 games with two singles off Lyons during the first game of a doubleheader on July 13 at Comiskey Park.

Upon joining the National League's Milwaukee Brewers for the 1999 season, pitcher Jim Abbott, who was born without a right hand, was required to bat in the big leagues for the first time. Abbott managed to collect two hits – both against Chicago's Jon Lieber. On June 15 at County Stadium, Abbott singled to left-center with two outs in the bottom of the fourth to score Sean Berry and give Milwaukee a 2-1 lead, but he would eventually take the loss when the Cubs rallied to win 7-4. On June 30 at Wrigley Field, Lieber intentionally walked Jose Valentin to pitch to Abbott with the bases loaded in the fourth, but Abbott spoiled the strategy with a two-run single to center. The Cubs won 5-4, and Abbott did not figure in the decision. Abbott was released by the Brewers in July and finished his hitting career 2 for 21 with three RBIs.

Boston's win at Yankee Stadium on May 2, 1995, is the only 8-0 major league game in which all eight runs resulted from grand slams – *and the slams were hit by players who were once college teammates.* John Valentin and Mo Vaughn, teammates at Seton Hall in 1987, accounted for all the Red Sox runs with Valentin's slam against Sterling Hitchcock in the third inning and Vaughn's slam off Brian Boehringer an inning later.

During his brief stay in Montreal, Pete Rose doubled against Philadelphia's Jerry Koosman during the fourth inning of Montreal's home opener on April 13, 1984, for his 4,000th career hit. Rose's milestone hit happened on the 21st anniversary of his first major league hit, a triple against Pittsburgh Pirate pitcher Bob Friend on April 13, 1963, at Crosley Field. Rose entered the game with 2,999 singles, so if he had singled, rather than doubled, his 4,000th hit would also have been his 3,000th single.

Hall of Fame second baseman Ryne Sandberg collected 2,385 of his 2,386 career hits for the Chicago Cubs, but his first major league hit came with the Philadelphia Phillies – *and he collected it against the Cubs at Wrigley Field.* Sandberg made his major league debut with the Phillies on September 2, 1981, and batted 13 times in six games. His lone hit as a Phillie was an eighth-inning single against Cubs' pitcher Mike Krukow on September 27, 1981. Following his January 27, 1982, trade to Chicago, Sandberg spent 15 years with the Cubs and also got his last hit at Wrigley Field – *this time against the Phillies.* On September 21, 1997, Sandberg singled to left in the fifth (and then left for a pinch runner) against Philadelphia's Curt Schilling in the same inning in which Schilling tied the National League season record for strikeouts by a righthanded pitcher. Four batters after Sandberg's single, Schilling fanned Brant Brown to tie J.R. Richard's record of 313 strikeouts.

On April 11, 1998, three major leaguers reached a milestone in a major statistical category. Mike Mussina recorded his 1,000th strikeout by fanning Bip Roberts looking in the sixth inning at Tiger Stadium, while Pedro Martinez reached the same milestone at Fenway Park when he whiffed Rick Wilkins to lead off the eighth. Although known for his enormous home runs, Mark McGwire got his 1,000th RBI when he walked with the bases loaded in the seventh against Shawn Estes.

Raul Mondesi's 1,000th career hit was also the last home run hit at Candlestick Park. Mondesi connected against Giants' hurler Mark Gardner with two men on in the sixth inning as San Francisco closed out their 40-year stay at Candlestick with a 9-4 loss to their longtime rivals, the Los Angeles Dodgers, on September 30, 1999.

Four members of the 500-home run club ended their career in the same city in which it began – *but with a different team.* All-time home run king Hank Aaron began with the Milwaukee Braves in 1954 and ended with the Milwaukee Brewers in 1976. Babe Ruth's career began in 1914 with the Boston Red Sox and came to an end with the Boston Braves in 1935. Willie Mays debuted with the Giants in 1951 when they were in New York and returned to finish with the New York Mets in 1973. Jimmie Foxx started in 1925 with the Philadelphia A's and finished up with the Philadelphia Phillies in 1945.

During their memorable home run duel in the 1998 season when Mark McGwire smashed a then record 70 homers and Sammy Sosa finished second with 66 long balls, they smacked their 64th home run *against the same pitcher.* McGwire's 64th four-bagger was a two-run shot in the fourth inning against Milwaukee's Rafael Roque at County Stadium on September 18. Five days later the Cubs visited County Stadium and Sosa hit two homers against the Brewers – the first of which was his 64th, a solo shot in the fifth against Roque.

Boston's Mike Greenwell hit two career inside-the-park home runs – *both against New York Yankees' pitcher Greg Cadaret at Fenway Park.* On July 7, 1989, with the score tied 4-4 in the sixth inning, Greenwell hit a shot off Cadaret toward the Green Monster in left field. Yankees' outfielder Roberto Kelly went back to make the catch, but the ball struck the base of the wall and bounced more than 100 feet away. Greenwell was waved around third and crashed into catcher Don Slaught just as the relay throw arrived at the plate. In the fifth inning on September 1, 1990, Greenwell collected a rare inside-the-park grand slam when he grounded a Cadaret pitch inside the first baseline and rounded the bases as right fielder Jesse Barfield slipped, injuring his knee, and allowed the ball to roll around the outfield wall.

During his days as a New York Yankee from 1938 to 1946, excluding 1944 and 1945 when he served in World War II, Joe Gordon appeared in exactly 1,000 games for the Yankees and collected exactly 1,000 hits.

Los Angeles Dodger pitchers Sandy Koufax and Don Drysdale each had 1,910 strikeouts during 1960s. Koufax recorded his strikeouts in 1,807.2 innings from 1960 to 1966, averaging 9.51 per nine innings and three times fanning over 300 hitters – including a then major league record 382 in 1965. Drysdale pitched the entire decade of the 1960s, whiffing his batters in 2,629.2 innings for an average of 6.54 per nine innings, with a career high of 251 in 1963.

Randy Johnson won his first two Cy Young Awards in 1995 and 1999 with a 2.48 ERA. Johnson won the award for the fourth time in 2001 when he pitched 249.2 innings and finished with an ERA of 2.49 – *just one additional out from an ERA of 2.48 again.*

Harvey Kuenn made the last out in two of Sandy Koufax's four no-hitters. On May 11, 1963, Kuenn ended Koufax's 8-0 no-hitter over the San Francisco Giants by bouncing back to the mound. Two seasons later on September 9, 1965, he was with the Chicago Cubs when he pinch-hit for pitcher Bob Hendley and struck out to end Koufax's perfect game.

Jose Mesa was on the mound when a number of career milestones were reached. Mesa allowed Robin Yount's 3,000th hit on September 9, 1992, served up Andre Dawson's 400th homer on April 15, 1993, and surrendered Ken Griffey, Jr.'s 300th home run on April 13, 1998. On April 25, 2001, Rickey Henderson coaxed a walk against Mesa to break Babe Ruth's record of 2,062 walks that had stood since 1935. Mesa also earned the last save at Cincinnati's Riverfront Stadium on September 22, 2002, when he got Todd Walker to ground out to end Philadelphia's 4-3 win over the Reds.

Craig Counsell played for the two fastest expansion teams to win the World Series – the 1997 Florida Marlins, who won in their fifth season, and the 2001 Arizona Diamondbacks, who won in just their fourth season. Counsell was involved in both final-inning rallies that decided the seventh game of each World Series. Despite being only 4 for 22 in the 1997 Series, he tied the score in the bottom of the ninth of Game 7 with a sacrifice fly to right field. In the 11th inning, Counsell reached on an error by second baseman Tony Fernandez and later scored the Series-winning run on Edgar Renteria's single as the Marlins beat the Cleveland Indians. In the 2001 Series against the Yankees, Counsell was just 2 for 24 but was hit by a pitch in the bottom of the ninth inning to load the bases and bring Luis Gonzalez to the plate. Gonzalez came through in the clutch with a bloop single over a drawn-in Derek Jeter at shortstop to score Jay Bell with the Series-winning run.

Hank Aaron and Babe Ruth, the top two home run hitters, are tied for third place on the all-time list of runs scored. Each scored 2,174 times.

Chan Ho Park was on the pitching end of some historic home runs. Park served up two grand slams to Fernando Tatis in the third inning on April 23, 1999, making Tatis the only player to hit two slams in a single inning. In the 2001 All-Star game at Safeco Field, the first batter Park faced in All-Star play was 40-year-old Cal Ripken, Jr. who homered against him to become the oldest player to hit an All-Star Game homer. On October 5, 2001, Park gave up Barry Bonds' record-breaking 71st home run in the first inning at Pac Bell Park and two innings later surrendered Bonds' 72nd.

The Angels went 16 years between playoff appearances – yet faced the *same* starting pitcher in consecutive playoff games. Boston's Roger Clemens beat them in Game 7 of the 1986 ALCS to advance the Red Sox to the World Series, and he got a no-decision as the Game 1 starter for New York when the Yankees faced the Angels in the 2002 ALDS.

Nolan Ryan was a member of the first playoff team for three different franchises – the Mets (1969), Angels (1979), and Astros (1980). Despite pitching in 27 seasons, Ryan only had one World Series appearance. In his third season with the Mets, he appeared in Game 3 of the 1969 Series in relief of starter Gary Gentry and pitched the final 2.1 innings, striking out three Orioles and earning the save.

Two members of the 500-homer club reached both a home run milestone and an RBI milestone in the same at-bat. Mel Ott raised his career RBIs total to 1,500 by hitting his 400th homer. He connected for a two-run shot in the bottom of the third against Monte Pearson at the Polo Grounds as the Giants beat the Reds 3-2 in the first game of a doubleheader on June 1, 1941. Rafael Palmeiro's 500th home run gave him exactly 1,600 RBIs. Palmeiro's blast came on May 11, 2003, and was a three-run shot off Dave Elder in the seventh inning at The Ballpark in Arlington in the Rangers' 17-10 victory over Cleveland.

Pitcher Jack Harper appeared in games for both the team with the most regular season wins and for the team with the most regular season losses. As a rookie, Harper pitched in five games for the 1899 Cleveland Spiders (20-134), winning one and losing four. His last appearance was a one inning, no-decision start for the 1906 Chicago Cubs (116-36).

Among all the men to play major league baseball, all-time home run king Hank Aaron is also the first hitter listed alphabetically among all the men who have played major league baseball. Upon playing his first game on April 13, 1954, Aaron became the first player – hitter or pitcher – on the list, but he was pushed down to second on April 6, 2004, when San Francisco pitcher David Aardsma made his major league debut.

Johnny Bench smacked 45 homers in 1970 to become the only catcher to lead either league in homers, a feat he duplicated with 40 more in 1972. During Bench's league-leading season in 1970 the Cincinnati Reds moved from Crosley Field and began playing at Riverfront Stadium on June 30. Bench hit 15 homers at Crosley before the move, hit 15 more in the Reds' new park, and hit his other 15 home runs on the road.

Teams from St. Louis have figured prominently in the championship seasons of Boston teams. The Boston Celtics won their first NBA championship by defeating the St. Louis Hawks in seven games in the 1957 NBA Finals. The New England Patriots won their first Super Bowl with a 20-17 win over the St. Louis Rams in Super Bowl XXXVI on February 3, 2002. The Boston Red Sox ended their 86-year World Series victory drought in 2004 with a four-game sweep of the St. Louis Cardinals.

On September 12, 2004, Ben Sheets squared off against the Cincinnati Reds. Brewers' third baseman Russell Branyan homered twice in support of Sheets, who cruised to an 11-0 win while striking out 11 hitters. The win evened Sheet's season record at 11-11 and tied his career high for wins – he had won exactly 11 games in each of his first three seasons (2001-2003).

Todd Zeile owns the MLB record of hitting a home run for the most different teams. His 253 lifetime homers were spread among 11 different teams – St. Louis (75), the Chicago Cubs (9), Philadelphia (20), Baltimore (5), Los Angeles (38), Florida (6), Texas (30), the New York Mets (41), Colorado (18), the New York Yankees (6) and Montreal (5). Zeile's final round-tripper was also the last homer given up by a Montreal Expo pitcher. In the last of his 7,573 major league at-bats, Zeile connected against Claudio Vargas in the sixth inning of New York's 8-1 victory over Montreal at Shea Stadium. The Expos moved to Washington, D.C. for the 2005 season and change their name to the Nationals.

On June 16, 1953, the St. Louis Browns won 3-1 to avoid setting a franchise-record losing steak – *and they did it by ending the New York Yankees' 18-game winning streak.* Following a perfect 14-game road trip, the Yankees returned home to face the lowly Browns, needing just one victory to match the longest winning streak in AL history. The Browns entered the game with 14 consecutive defeats – including four to the Yankees during their winning streak – which tied the team mark set in 1911 and 1940. The pitching match-up was young Whitey Ford against Duane Pillette, who was seeking just his second win of the year. The Browns got on the board in the second inning with walks to Les Moss and Pillette followed by an RBI single by Johnny Groth. Vic Wertz made the score 3-0 when he homered off Ford in the fifth. New York avoided being blanked by scoring their lone run in the fifth inning on a pinch-hit single by Johnny Mize, his 2,000th career hit. Pillette worked into the eighth and then was relieved by Satchel Paige who got the last five outs. The loss was the first for Ford as a Yankee starter. The Yankees rebounded to sweep the next three games of the series on their way to a 17-5 record against the Browns in 1953.

In 1961 when the New York Yankees' Roger Maris hit 61 homers and Mickey Mantle hit 54, they each finished with just 16 doubles – the fewest by any player with 50 or more homers in a season.

Fergie Jenkins and Greg Maddux are the only pitchers to strike out over 3,000 batters while walking fewer than 1,000 – *and each recorded his 3,000th career strikeout with the Chicago Cubs while wearing uniform #31.* Jenkins picked up his milestone strikeout against Garry Templeton at San Diego on May 25, 1982, and finished his 19-year career in 1983 with 284 wins, 3,192 strikeouts and 997 walks. Maddux fanned Giants' shortstop Omar Vizquel at Wrigley Field on July 26, 2005, for his 3,000th whiff and had 318 wins, 3,052 strikeouts, and 907 walks entering the 2006 season. Maddux's 300th win on August 7, 2004, was also against the Giants, making him the only pitcher to get his 300th win and 3,000th strikeout against the same team.

The first Hall of Fame plaques depicting players wearing hats of the Texas Rangers, Kansas City Royals, and Milwaukee Brewers were all added in the same year. Nolan Ryan, Robin Yount, and George Brett were each elected to Cooperstown in 1999 in their first year of eligibility. Ryan pitched his last five seasons in Texas and chose to be shown wearing a Ranger hat on his plaque. Yount spent his entire 20-year career with the Brewers, and Brett played all 21 of his seasons with the Royals.

Debuts

Ron Wright's major league career consisted of just one game and three at-bats – *but he managed to hit into a triple play, a double play and strike out.* Pressed into service as the Seattle DH on April 14, 2002, when Jeff Cirillo was injured by a stray ball during batting practice, Wright struck out in his first major league at-bat against Texas pitcher Kenny Rogers with two runners on base. In the fourth inning, Wright came to the plate with Ruben Sierra on third and John Olerud on first and grounded back to the mound. Rogers fielded the ball, threw to second base to force Olerud, and then shortstop Alex Rodriguez fired to the plate, catching Sierra in a rundown. Rogers eventually tagged out Sierra and threw to second baseman Michael Young, who tagged Wright as he tried to advance to second base. In his final big league at-bat, Wright grounded into a 6-4-3 double play in the sixth inning.

Ben Grieve made his major league debut on September 3, 1997, by collecting three doubles – *in three consecutive innings against three different pitchers.* In the sixth inning of the A's 12-3 win over San Francisco, Grieve doubled in a run against Danny Darwin and followed with a seventh-inning, bases-loaded two-bagger against Jim Poole. He later added an RBI double against Cory Bailey in the eighth to finish his first major league game 3 for 4 with five RBIs and a walk.

Before he threw a single pitch, future Hall of Fame pitcher Greg Maddux made his big league appearance *as a pinch runner.* Because

Wrigley Field did not have lights at the time, the Chicago game against Houston (started by future 300-game winner Nolan Ryan) on September 2, 1986, was suspended due to darkness after 14 innings with the scored tied 4-4. The game resumed the following day with the Astros pushing across three runs in the 17th, only to see the Cubs tie the game again on a three-run homer from Keith Moreland. Following Moreland's blast, Maddux ran for catcher Jody Davis who had singled. The Cubs did not score again so Maddux stayed in to pitch and surrendered a one-out homer to Billy Hatcher in the 18th inning and was the losing pitcher when the Cubs failed to score in the bottom of the frame. The game featured a National League record for total players (53) used in an extra-inning game.

John Paciorek's career consisted of only one game. His lone big league appearance was in right field for the Houston Colt .45s on September 29, 1963, the last day of the season. Paciorek made the most of his opportunity by having a perfect day at the plate, getting three hits and two walks in five trips. He also knocked in three runs and scored four times. Although Paciorek was only 18 years old when played his first game, he never made it back to the majors. Back problems bothered Paciorek during his entire career, and he retired after a few more injury-plagued seasons in the minors – with the most hits of any player with a 1.000 batting average in the major leagues.

John Sipin's brief major league career (229 at-bats with the 1969 San Diego Padres) began with a bang – he tripled in his first two at-bats, making him the only player to do so. On May 24 at Jack Murphy Stadium, Sipin made his debut and tripled to left field in the first inning and to center field to lead off the fourth, both times against Cub pitcher Ken Holtzman. They were the only two triples among his 51 career hits.

Pitcher Larry Yount, brother of Hall of Fame player Robin Yount, is credited with one game played in the majors – *although he never threw a pitch*. Houston brought Yount in to make his major league debut against the Atlanta Braves in the top of the ninth on

September 15, 1971. After he had officially been announced into the game, Yount hurt his arm while warming up and was replaced before throwing a single pitch. He was sent back to the minors and eventually retired without ever making it back to the big leagues.

On August 1, 1985, the Minnesota Twins traded minor leaguer Jay Bell and three other players to the Cleveland Indians for veteran pitcher Bert Blyleven. More than a year later, on September 29, 1986, Bell made his major league debut in the Metrodome and hit a home run on the first pitch thrown to him – *a pitch thrown by Bert Blyleven.* Bell's homer was the 47th of the year against Blyleven, breaking Robin Roberts' 1956 record for the most home runs allowed in a season. Blyleven ended the season with 50 homers allowed and then surrendered another 46 homers in 1987.

On April 19, opening day of the 1938 season, Heinie Mueller of the Phillies and Ernie Koy of the Dodgers each homered in his first major league at-bat – *in the same inning.* Koy hit a solo homer in the top of the first at the Baker Bowl against Wayne LaMaster to give Brooklyn an early lead, but Mueller led off the bottom of the first and quickly tied the game with a shot off Van Mungo. Koy added a double and a single while Mueller had another single and scored two more runs as Brooklyn won 12-5.

Brad Hennessey lost his major league debut on August 7, 2004, at San Francisco – *to Greg Maddux who won his 300th career game.* Hennessey pitched 4.2 innings, giving up seven hits and four earned runs. Maddux struggled with his control but left with a 6-3 lead in the sixth with two men on base and nobody out. The Cubs' bullpen came through and shut the Giants down, and the Cubs eventually won 8-4. The last time a pitcher won his 300th game against a pitcher who was making his major league debut was on July 12, 1901, when Cy Young beat John McPherson.

Ted Cox set a major league record by getting six consecutive hits to start his career. He went 4 for 4 in his first game with the Boston Red Sox on September 18, 1977, when they beat the Orioles 10-4 at Memorial Stadium. Batting second in the lineup against Baltimore starter Mike Flanagan, Cox singled in the first, walked and scored his first run in the third, and singled and scored again in the fifth. In the sixth inning he collected his first RBI with a single to center against Scott McGregor and then finished off his perfect day with a two-base hit against McGregor in the ninth. The next day at Fenway Park against the Yankees, Cox singled the first two times he faced starter Ed Figueroa before he was finally retired on a ground ball to first baseman Chris Chambliss.

Acquired in a trade with the Phillies just two days earlier, Don Cardwell made his first start for the Cubs on May 15, 1960, and threw a no-hitter against the St. Louis Cardinals at Wrigley Field. Following the Cubs' 6-1 loss in the first game of a doubleheader, Cardwell took the mound and faced just 28 batters, retiring the last 26 in succession. The Cardinals' lone baserunner was a one-out walk to shortstop Alex Grammas in the first. Cardwell's pitching gem ended with a spectacular play by Cubs' left fielder Walt Moryn who charged in to make a shoestring catch of Joe Cunningham's sinking line drive and, without breaking stride, raced to the mound to join in congratulating Cardwell on his pitching feat.

Jim McAndrew began his pitching career by suffering losses *in four consecutive shutouts.* McAndrew made his debut on July 21, 1968, against the Cardinals at St. Louis. He struck out five and allowed just one run, an inside-the-park homer to Bobby Tolan to lead off the sixth, but the Mets lost 2-0 to Bob Gibson. McAndrew allowed two runs in 4.2 inning in his next start on August 4 at Los Angeles, but his opponent Mike Kekich pitched brilliantly, throwing a one-hit, 11-strikeout masterpiece to beat the Mets 2-0. His third start was six days later against the Giants in San Francisco where he pitched seven innings, giving up an RBI single to Bob Barton in the sixth, and lost 1-0 to Bobby Bolin, who threw a four-hit, nine-strikeout gem. McAndrew lost his home debut 1-0 on August 17 against Houston despite allowing just a single run in seven innings, his only mistake being a sixth-inning homer to Jim Wynn. After four solid outings, McAndrew was hammered for six earned runs in 4.2 innings of a 13-3 loss to Juan Marichal and the Giants in his next start. He finally tasted victory when he beat Steve Carlton and the Cardinals with a complete-game, 1-0 performance on August 26 in his sixth start. However, the next time out on August 31, McAndrew suffered yet another shutout loss when he pitched eight solid innings but was beaten 2-0 by Carlton and St. Louis.

Jeremy Hermida's major league career began with a bang when he became the only player to hit a pinch-hit grand slam in his *first career at-bat*. With the Marlins trailing the Cardinals 10-0 in the bottom of the seventh inning on August 31, 2005, Hermida was summoned to bat for Brian Moehler. Facing reliever Al Reyes, he swung and missed, took a ball, and then homered into the right field stands on the third pitch. Hermida's blast made him just the third player to hit a grand slam in his first game, joining pitcher Bill Duggleby (in his first at-bat for Philadelphia on April 21, 1898) and Bobby Bonds (in his third at-bat for San Francisco on June 25, 1968).

Alejandro Machado scored his first major league run on September 14, 2005, on a home run by Tony Graffanino – *although Machado was not even on base when the homer was hit*. With Boston trailing 2-1 at Toronto, Red Sox outfielder Gabe Kapler reached first on an error by Blue Jay third baseman Corey Koskie. Graffanino followed with a homer to left. Kapler, unsure if the ball would clear the fence, raced to second and ruptured his left Achilles' tendon after rounding the base. After a five-minute delay, Kapler was carted off the field and Machado was summoned to second base to pinch-run. He completed Kapler's trip around the bases, followed by Graffanino who had waited near second during the delay. It was Machado's fourth big league appearance – *and his first time on base*.

Mike Bordick signed with Toronto as a free agent and played his first game with the Blue Jays on April 2, 2003. Bordick began the contest with active streaks of 110 consecutive errorless games and 543 straight chances without an error – both major league records for a shortstop – but made a miscue on just his *second* chance with his new team. Bordick's streaks ended in the top of the third when he let Bubba Trammell's ground ball kick off his glove for an error.

Jon Nunnally stole six bases in ten attempts in his rookie year of 1995 – *the last four steals of which were steals of home.* After two unsuccessful stolen base attempts, the Kansas City speedster swiped his first two bases against Toronto on May 24 and got his first career steal of home the next night against the Blue Jays. Nunnally was unsuccessful in an attempted steal of home against Oakland on June 18 but got his second swipe of the plate on July 29 against Detroit. He also proved that he could do more than run by ending the game with a solo homer in the 16th inning against Detroit's John Doherty – the Royals' *first* extra-base hit of the game after 21 straight singles. Nunnally's final steals of home came in a rain-shortened, 7-4 win against Oakland on August 15 and a 16-7 victory over Minnesota on September 18. Nunnally finished his six-year career in 2000 with 19 career stolen bases, including one more steal of home with Cincinnati on September 14, 1997, against Philadelphia.

Family

The three Alou brothers played special roles in the opening game of three different ballparks. On April 12, 1966, Pittsburgh's Matty Alou was the first batter at Atlanta's Fulton County Stadium in the top of the first and his brother, Felipe, was the first Brave to bat in the bottom of the first. St. Louis opened Busch Memorial Stadium one month later on May 12, and this time Felipe was the first batter. He hit two homers in the game, including the park's first one against Ray Washburn in the sixth. Their brother, Jesus, was the first batter at San Diego Stadium (later Jack Murphy Stadium) on April 8, 1969, and singled to right field for the first hit. More than 30 years after his father was the first Braves' player to bat at Fulton County Stadium, Felipe's son, Moises, was the park's last regular season batter on September 23, 1996.

Dixie and Harry Walker are the only brothers to each win a batting title. Dixie led the NL in 1944 when he hit .357 for Brooklyn. Harry led the NL in 1947 with a .363 average while splitting the season between St. Louis (ten games) and Philadelphia (130 games).

Hall of Fame brothers Paul and Lloyd Waner played together on three different clubs. Paul began his career with the Pittsburgh Pirates in 1926. Lloyd joined him the next season, and they remained Pirate teammates through the 1940 season. Paul began the 1941 season with Brooklyn with Lloyd still in Pittsburgh, but they were soon reunited on the Boston Braves. Paul appeared in 95 games for the Braves while Lloyd played in 19 games before finishing the season with Cincinnati. In 1944 they teamed up again, this time both starting the season with the Brooklyn Dodgers. Paul played 83 games as a Dodger that season, and Lloyd appeared in 15.

Bobby Bonds and his son Barry share the record of five seasons with 30 homers and 30 steals. Bobby had 30-30 seasons for San Francisco in 1969 and 1973, the New York Yankees in 1975, and the California Angels in 1977. He also had 31 homers and 43 steals in the 1978 season while splitting time between Chicago White Sox and Texas Rangers. Barry had two 30-30 seasons with Pittsburgh (1990 and 1992) and three more with San Francisco (1995-1997). New York Mets' third baseman Howard Johnson (1987, 1989, and 1991) is the only other player with more than two seasons of 30 homers and 30 steals.

Dizzy Dean and his brother, Paul, accounted for all four St. Louis wins during the Cardinals' 1934 World Series victory over the Detroit Tigers. Dizzy won the opener in Detroit by an 8-3 score. Following a Detroit win in Game 2, Paul held the Tigers to one run and won Game 3 by a 4-1 count. Following Dizzy's 3-1 loss to the Tigers in Game 5, Paul came back beat the Tigers 4-3 to tie the Series at three games each. Dizzy returned in Game 7 and shut out the Tigers 11-0 to win the World Series for St. Louis. The Dean brothers combined to pitch 44 innings, giving up only seven earned runs, and strike out 28 batters.

Joe Niekro's only major league home run came on May 29, 1976, in the seventh inning at Atlanta's Fulton County Stadium – *against his brother Phil*. Joe's homer helped the Astros to 4-3 win over the Braves. In 1979 the Niekro brothers tied for the National League lead with 21 wins each. They went head-to-head on September 26 with Phil and the Braves beating Joe's Astros 9-4 at Fulton County Stadium to even up their victory totals at 20 each. On September 30, the last day of the season, each won his 21st game as Phil beat the Reds 7-2 at Riverfront Stadium and Joe edged the Dodgers 3-2 in Los Angeles. Joe finished 21-11 with a 3.00 ERA, while Phil was 21-20 with a 3.39 ERA.

Ken Griffey, Sr. and Ken Griffey, Jr. are the only father and son to homer in the same game. On September 14, 1990, Griffey, Sr. belted a two-run home run in the top of the first inning against Angels' pitcher Kirk McCaskill. Batting next, Griffey, Jr. also homered against McCaskill. While Junior would hit many more homers, Senior would only hit one more before retiring in 1991. The only other instance of a father and son playing together occurred at the end of 2001 when Tim Raines was sent to Baltimore so that he could appear in the final four games of the year with his son, Tim Jr. The elder Raines batted 3 for 11 and Tim, Jr. was 3 for 16, but they did not get hits in the same game. The Griffeys are also the only father-son combination to each win the All-Star MVP Award. In the 1980 game at Los Angeles, the NL won 4-2 as Griffey, Sr. help them overcome a 2-0 deficit with two hits, including a solo homer (the first NL hit) against Tommy John in the fifth. Griffey, Jr. matched his father's feat in the 1992 game in San Diego when he banged out three hits, including a double and a homer against Greg Maddux, and led the AL to a 13-6 victory.

Pat Underwood made his major league pitching debut by going head-to-head against his older brother, Tom, at Toronto's Exhibition Stadium on May 31, 1979. Pat gave up just three hits and fanned four in 8.1 innings to get the win by a 1-0 score. Tom pitched all nine innings, surrendering just six hits to go with six strikeouts, but Jerry Morales homered on his first pitch in the eighth inning to break the scoreless duel and provide the game's only run.

Through the 2001 season, Von Hayes was the only player to homer twice in the first inning of a game (June 11, 1985), but then it was accomplished by three more players by the end of the 2002 season – including by brothers Bret and Aaron Boone. On May 2 in a 15-4 win at Comiskey Park, Bret and his Mariner teammate, Mike Cameron, each homered in the first inning against both Jon Rauch and Jim Parque. Cameron would hit two more homers to tie the major league record of four in one game. On August 9 in Cincinnati's 12-10 win at Riverfront Stadium, Aaron Boone hit three homers against Brett Tomko, including two in the opening frame.

Through the 2003 season, no members of the same family had ever each hit for the cycle – *but then it happened twice in just over a month.* Pittsburgh's Daryle Ward cycled on May 26, 2004, at Busch Stadium, making him and his father, Gary, the only father-son combination to each collect a cycle. Gary Ward had done it for the Minnesota Twins on September 18, 1980, at County Stadium. On June 28, 2004, David Bell hit for the cycle against the Montreal Expos, making him and his grandfather, Gus, the only grandfather-grandson combination to accomplish the feat. Gus Bell's cycle came with Pittsburgh against Philadelphia on June 4, 1951.

On September 6, 2002, pitchers Andy and Alan Benes squared off against each other at Busch Stadium, and Andy collected two hits against his younger brother *in one inning.* The game was scoreless when Andy led off with a single to left in the bottom of the third. The Cardinals batted around, and later in the inning Andy added an RBI single to center to knock his brother from the game. Andy pitched a complete game, striking out six, as the Cardinals won 11-2.

Matty Alou won the 1966 National League batting race with a .342 average for the Pittsburgh Pirates, finishing ahead of his brother Felipe who came in second with a .327 average for the Atlanta Braves. Their younger brother, Jesus, batted .259 for the San Francisco Giants. On September 22, 1963, the Alou brothers made major league history by appearing in the outfield together in the Giants' 13-4 win over New York at Candlestick Park. In the seventh inning, Matty replaced Willie Mays and played left field, with Felipe shifting to center field and Jesus sliding over to right.

Bob and Ken Forsch are the only pair of brothers to each hurl an official no-hitter. Bob threw two no-hitters for the Cardinals at Busch Stadium. His first no-hitter was a 5-0 victory against the Phillies on April 16, 1978, and the other was a 3-0 gem against Montreal on September 26, 1983. Ken pitched his no-hitter in his first start of the 1979 season, leading Houston to a 6-0 win over Atlanta at the Astrodome on April 7. Pascual Perez and his brother, Melido, each pitched rained-shortened, *unofficial* no-hitters. Pascual held the Phillies without a hit as Montreal won 1-0 in a five-inning game on September 24, 1988, at Veterans Stadium. Melido pitched the White Sox to an 8-0 victory at Yankee Stadium on September 20, 1990, but lost his chance at a no-hitter when the game was called with Chicago batting in the top of the seventh.

Mike Schmidt is the only player to homer against a pair of brothers during a four-homer game. On April 17, 1976, the Phillies beat the Cubs in a wild game at Wrigley Field. The Cubs jumped to an early 12-1 lead, but Schmidt smashed a two-run homer off Cubs' starter Rick Reuschel with one out in the fifth to make the score 13-4. Schmidt hit a solo homer off Reuschel in the seventh to make the score 13-7 and a three-run blast with two outs in the eighth against Mike Garman to pull the Phillies within one run at 13-12. Philadelphia plated three more in the ninth to take a 15-13 lead, but Chicago rallied in the bottom of the frame to force extra innings. Following a lead-off walk to Dick Allen in the 10th, Schmidt homered against Paul Reuschel to give his team a 17-15 edge, their first lead since it was 1-0 in the second inning. The Phillies would add one more run and hold on for an 18-16 win.

Golden Oldies

Sam Rice had six 200-hit seasons – *all after he turned 30 years old*. Rice came to the Senators in 1915 as a pitcher but was eventually moved to the outfield in the middle of the 1916 season and did not play his first full season in the field until 1917 at the age of 27. He then spent most of 1918 in the army, appearing in just seven games. Rice turned 30 on February 20, 1920, and had his first 200-hit season that year. He then topped the 200-hit mark five more times (1924, 1925, 1926, 1928 and 1930) and came close in 1929 when he finished with 199 hits. Rice's 207 hits in 1930 make him the only player over the age of 40 to have a 200-hit season. Paul Molitor finished the 1996 season with 225 hits, but he celebrated his 40th birthday on August 22 during the season. Rice's career ended after his 1934 season with the Indians when he banged out 98 hits to finish with 2,987 hits, just short of the 3,000 mark.

Nolan Ryan led each league in strikeouts twice – *after he turned 40 years old*. In his last two years with the Houston Astros, Ryan led the National League with 270 strikeouts at age 40 in 1987 and again with 228 whiffs the following year. Moving to the American League with the Texas Rangers for the 1989 season, Ryan led the league with 301 strikeouts and followed by whiffing a league-leading 232 batters in 1990.

Phil Niekro won 287 games and struck out 2,999 batters – *after the age of 30*. He turned 30 on April 1, 1969, and entered the season with a record of 31-27 and 343 strikeouts. Niekro's knuckleball allowed him to pitch until 1987 when he retired at age 48 with a record of 318-274 and 3,342 strikeouts. On the last day of the 1985 season Niekro went the distance, allowing four hits and three walks and striking out five, to beat the Blue Jays 8-0 and win his 300th career game. The victory also made him, at age 46, the oldest pitcher to throw a shutout.

Jack Quinn is both the oldest pitcher to start a World Series game and the oldest pitcher to win a major league game. The 45-year-old hurler started Game 4 of the 1929 Series for the Philadelphia A's, giving up six runs (five earned) and seven hits in five innings. He did not figure in the decision because the A's staged the largest rally in World Series history by scoring ten in the bottom of the seventh to erase the Cubs' 8-0 lead. Quinn also appeared in the World Series the following season, pitching the final two innings of the A's Game 3 loss to the St. Louis Cardinals. In 1932 Quinn appeared in 42 games in relief for the Brooklyn Dodgers, compiling a 3-7 record with a 3.31 ERA in 87 innings. His last win came on September 13 – just over two months past his 49th birthday – when he threw the final five frames of the Dodgers' 6-5, ten-inning win over the Cardinals at Ebbets Field. Quinn pitched in 14 games for the Cincinnati Reds the next season, recording just one decision – a loss to the Dodgers on June 28 – and ended his career with a record of 247-218. Entering the 2006 season, Quinn is also the oldest player to hit a home run. On June 27, 1930, at the age of 46 years and 357 days, Quinn clouted the last of his eight career homers in the sixth inning at Shibe Park against Browns' pitcher Chad Kimsey, who earlier in the game had served up long balls to Hall of Fame sluggers Jimmie Foxx and Al Simmons. Quinn's record as the oldest player to homer will be broken if 47-year-old Julio Franco connects once during the 2006 season.

When pitcher Randy Johnson connected for his first major league homer on September 19, 2003, it made him the oldest player to homer for the first time. Johnson was 40 years and 9 days old when he took Milwaukee's Doug Davis deep at Miller Park in the top of the third. His blast gave him a 1-0 lead, but he eventually got a no-decision in Arizona's 3-2 win over the Brewers.

Houston's Roger Clemens (age 42) and Arizona's Randy Johnson (age 41) finished first and second in the 2004 National League Cy Young voting – *making them both older than the previous oldest pitcher to win the award.* Gaylord Perry had been the oldest pitcher to win the Cy Young award when he went 21-6 for San Diego in 1978 and turned 40 just before the season ended. Clemens won a record seventh Cy Young – and his first in the National League – by finishing the season 18-4 with a 2.98 ERA and 218 strikeouts. Johnson, a five-time Cy Young Award winner, was just 16-14 because the Diamondbacks scored two runs or fewer in 17 of his 35 starts, but he had a 2.60 ERA and a major league-leading 290 strikeouts. Johnson's 16 wins for a Diamondback team that finished 51-111 gave him the most wins ever for a pitcher whose team lost 110 or more games.

Starting at the age of 36, Braves' lefthander Warren Spahn led the National League in complete games for a record *seven* consecutive seasons (1957-1963). Spahn led the league outright each of those seasons except for 1960 when he tied with Lew Burdette and Vern Law. Spahn also led the NL in complete games in 1949 and 1951 and finished second in five other seasons (1947, 1950, 1953, 1954, and 1956).

Willie Mays walked 1,464 times but led the National League only once – *and it was when he was 40 years old.* Mays topped the NL with 112 walks for the 1971 San Francisco Giants, the only time he ever reached the 100-walk mark in a season. Mays would walk only 87 more times before retiring following the 1973 World Series.

Dave Winfield and Harold Baines are the only players to knock in 100 runs in a season after they turned 40 years old. Winfield drove in 108 runs for the 1992 Toronto Blue Jays. Baines knocked in 103 runs in 1999, getting 81 RBIs in 107 games with Baltimore and 22 more in 28 games after being traded to Cleveland. Paul Molitor (1996) and Barry Bonds (2004) each drove in over 100 runs *during* the season in which they turned 40. Baines' 100-RBI season in 1999 was his first since 1985 when he knocked in 113 for the Chicago White Sox and broke Willie Horton's record for the longest span between 100-RBI seasons.

Johnny Bench hit his last home run on "Johnny Bench Night" at Riverfront Stadium on September 17, 1983. Following an emotional pre-game ceremony to honor his 17 years with the Reds, the Hall of Fame catcher made just his third start of the season behind the plate. Bench led off the third inning against Houston's Mike Madden and drilled the second pitch over the left field wall for his 389th career homer and tied the game at 2-2. Bench also collected a single and a walk, but the Astros won 4-3.

At age 38, Darrell Evans hit 40 homers for the 1985 Detroit Tigers, making him the oldest player to win a home run title. Evans' league-leading season was his first 40-homer season since he hit 41 for the 1973 Atlanta Braves, and it made him the first player to hit 40 in each league. His 12-year gap between 40-homer seasons is a major league record.

During the 2004 and 2005 seasons, Julio Franco set several home run marks. Born August 23, 1958, Franco became the oldest player to deliver a pinch-hit homer, breaking Deacon McGuire's record set on July 25, 1907, when he went deep against Brian Lawrence of San Diego on May 6, 2004. It was also the *first* pinch-hit homer of his 20-year career, but he would hit his second just 11 days against Arizona's Jose Valverde. During the first inning of Atlanta's 8-4 win against Philadelphia on June 3, Franco broke Carlton Fisk's record for the oldest player to hit a grand slam when he connected on the first pitch against Josh Hancock of the Reds. The next season on June 18, 2005, Franco hit a solo homer in the first and a two-run shot in the third against Cincinnati's Eric Milton to become the oldest player with a two-homer game. Just nine days later, at the age of 46 years and 308 days, Franco broke two of his own records with a *pinch-hit grand slam* against Valerio de los Santos of Florida in the eighth inning of a rain-shortened, 7-2 Atlanta win. Franco's last homer of 2005 was on August 13, giving him nine for the season and leaving him just short of Jack Quinn's record as the oldest man to hit a home run of any type – a record that Franco will shatter with his first homer of the 2006 season. Through the 2002 season, no player at the age of 44 or older had ever produced a five-homer season – but then Franco did it *three consecutive years*, with totals of five, six, and nine homers from 2003 to 2005.

On September 30, 1934, Charley O'Leary collected his last big league hit – more than *21 years* after his previous hit. O'Leary, a lifetime .226 hitter, was just days shy of his 52nd birthday when he was coaching with the St. Louis Browns in a meaningless doubleheader on the last day of the season. He persuaded the team to let him pinch-hit for pitcher George Blaeholder in the sixth inning of the second game, and he singled against 24-year-old Detroit pitcher Elden Auker and eventually scoring the Browns' first run in their 6-2 loss to the Tigers.

Home Run Feats

At age 35, and after 12 years with the Phillies and two with the Cubs, Hall of Fame center fielder Richie Ashburn joined the expansion New York Mets for the 1962 season at the Polo Grounds. At that time the light-hitting outfielder had just 22 career home runs, seven of which were inside-the-park, but he had taken advantage of the cozy Polo Grounds' foul lines and its vast center field to hit eight homers there as a visiting player – *more than the six he hit at Shibe Park in his 12 years with the Phillies.* In 1962 with the Polo Grounds as his home field, he would hit a career-best seven homers in his last season. After not homering in his two seasons with the Cubs, Ashburn's first homer with the Mets came against the Cubs at Wrigley Field on June 16 and was his first homer since July 2, 1959. On June 23 against Houston, he topped his previous career-high of four homers when he homered twice, including his last inside-the-parker. It was only the second two-homer game of his career with the other also coming at the Polo Grounds on April 28, 1956. Ashburn ended his career with only 29 home runs among his 2,574 hits. His power surge in his final season kept him from having the fewest homers by a player with more than 2,500 hits, edging him past Rabbit Maranville who hit 28 four-baggers among his 2,605 hits from 1912 to 1935.

Cal Ripken, Jr. homered in the game before he tied Lou Gehrig's record consecutive game streak and in the games that tied and broke Gehrig's mark. Playing in his 2,129th consecutive game, Ripken's third-inning homer run against Jim Abbott broke a string of 23 straight homerless games for the Oriole shortstop. The next night Ripken tied Gehrig at 2,130 straight games and celebrated by homering to lead off the sixth inning against California lefthander Mark Holzemer. The next night, September 6, 1995, as he broke a record that many fans thought would never be broken, Ripken swatted a pitch from Angels' pitcher Shawn Boskie into the left field stands to lead off the fourth inning.

Only two of the 12 players who hit two grand slams in a single game were National Leaguers – Atlanta pitcher Tony Cloninger and St. Louis third baseman Fernando Tatis. Cloninger became the only pitcher to hit two slams in a game when he connected twice against the San Francisco Giants at Candlestick Park on July 3, 1966. The first slam came off Bob Priddy in the opening inning and was followed by another in the fourth against Ray Sadecki. They were the only two grand slams among his 11 career home runs. Cloninger later added a single in the eighth for his ninth RBI of the game. Tatis is the only player to hit both of his slams in the same inning. He smacked two grand slams in the third inning of the Cardinals game against the Dodgers on April 23, 1999, at Dodger Stadium. Both slams came against Chan Ho Park, and the eight runs that Tatis drove in set the record for most RBIs in one inning.

Pitching legend Nolan Ryan hit just two home runs in 852 at-bats in his career, but he made them both count – *each was a three-run homer.* Ryan's first was a fourth-inning blast at the Astrodome against Hall of Fame pitcher Don Sutton on April 12, 1980, in a game that the Astros would eventually lose 6-5 in 17 innings. His second long ball came off Charlie Puleo in the seventh inning of a 12-3 rout of the Braves in Atlanta on May 1, 1987.

Don Mattingly set a major league record in 1987 by hitting six grand slams – *the only six grand slams of his 14-year career.* Mattingly's slams against Chicago's Joel McKeon on July 10 at Yankee Stadium and Texas knuckleballer Charlie Hough on July 16 at Arlington Stadium were part of his streak of eight consecutive games with a homer – a feat that tied the major league record set by Pittsburgh's Dale Long in 1956.

Since the 1920s, the only decade that did not produce a player with 50 homers in a season was the 1980s. Led by Mark McGwire's four consecutive 50-homer seasons from 1996 to 1999, the 1990s featured the most, with seven players combining for 12 seasons of 50+ homers.

There have been three instances where a pair of sluggers reached home run milestones on the same day. On May 8, 1998, Mark McGwire launched his 400th career home run when he connected in the third inning against Rick Reed at Shea Stadium and Andres Galarraga hit his 300th homer against Padres' pitcher Andy Ashby in the seventh at Atlanta's Turner Field. Both Albert Belle and Rafael Palmeiro hit their 300th home run on July 17, 1998. Belle smashed his homer at Comiskey Park in the sixth inning against Cleveland's Charles Nagy, while Palmeiro went deep in the eighth against Angel hurler Greg Cadaret at Anaheim Stadium. On June 5, 2002, Juan Gonzalez hit his 400th career long ball against Jarrod Washburn in the second inning at Anaheim and Jim Thome connected for his 300th against Eric Milton at Minnesota.

John Miller hit only two home runs in 61 career at-bats – *and they came in his first and last at-bats.* Miller debuted with the New York Yankees on September 11, 1966, and hit a two-run homer at Fenway Park against Boston pitcher Lee Stange. After a stint in the minors, Miller caught on with the Dodgers for the 1969 season and, even though he did not know it at the time, homered in his last major league at-bat when he pinch-hit and smacked a solo homer off Cincinnati's Jim Merritt on September 23, 1969.

Robin Ventura retired following the 2004 season with 18 career grand slams among his 294 homers – *as the only player with 13 or more grand slams who did not hit at least 300 career homers.* Ventura is currently fourth on the all-time list behind only Lou Gehrig (23), Manny Ramirez (20 through 2005) and Eddie Murray (19). On two occasions Ventura smashed two grand slams in one day, and each of the four blasts came with two men out. In the White Sox 14-3 victory at Texas on September 4, 1995, he became one of just 12 big leaguers to hit two slams in one game when he connected against Dennis Cook in the fourth and Danny Darwin in the fifth. Ventura led the New York Mets to a sweep of the Milwaukee Brewers at County Stadium on May 20, 1999, by becoming the only player to hit a grand slam in each game of a doubleheader. He opened the first game with a slam in the first inning against Jim Abbott and added a fourth-inning slam in the second game against Horacio Estrada. Ventura finished his career with the Los Angeles Dodgers in 2004 and hit just five homers – but the last two were grand slams. On August 29 at New York, he smashed a fifth-inning slam off Mets' pitcher Kris Benson. His last grand slam came on September 7 at Dodger Stadium when he pinch-hit against Arizona's Chad Durbin.

On his way to 66 home runs and the 1998 National League MVP, Sammy Sosa set a major league record by blasting 20 homers in a single month. Sosa ended May with 13 homers and then went on a home run binge in June. The Cubs' slugger started with a two-homer game on June 1 against Florida and then had three more multi-homer games – he hit three on June 15 against Milwaukee's Cal Eldred, two against Philadelphia's Carlton Loewer on June 19, and two more against the Phillies on June 20. Sosa hit 16 of his 20 homers at the Friendly Confines of Wrigley Field, including all four multi-homer games. The other four home runs were hit at Minnesota, Philadelphia, and Detroit (two).

A rainout prevented Ken Griffey, Jr. from matching Mark McGwire as the first player to hit 50 or more home runs in three consecutive seasons. Griffey lost a homer and two RBIs when his first-inning blast against Jack McDowell at Jacobs Field on September 6, 1996, was washed away when the game was halted in the top of the fourth inning. Griffey finished the 1996 season with 49 homers and then posted back-to-back seasons of 56 homers.

Despite 512 career homers, Eddie Mathews had just one three-homer game – which came in the Braves' last win while in Boston. On September 27, 1952, the 20-year-old rookie hit three homers against Brooklyn at Ebbets Field, leading the Braves to an 11-3 win. After striking out in the first, Mathews homered off Joe Black in the third and then against Ben Wade in the sixth and eighth before grounding out on a 3-0 pitch in the ninth. The next day's game, the last for the Braves in Boston before their move to Milwaukee, was suspended due to darkness after 12 innings with the two teams were tied 5-5.

After hitting just *one* homer from 1992 to 1995 and later sitting out the entire 1999 season, Kevin Elster smacked three home runs in the first game at San Francisco's Pac Bell Park on April 11, 2000. Elster connected in the third and fifth innings against Kirk Rueter and in the eighth against Felix Rodriguez, leading the Dodgers to a 6-5 win. Elster would swat three more long balls in April 2000 but then not hit three homers in *any other month* during the rest of the 2000 season and end his career at the end of the year with just 88 homers.

In the 1999 season, Houston's Jeff Bagwell had two three-homer games in Chicago – *but in different ballparks*. Bagwell lit up the Cubs for three homers and matched his career high of six RBIs at Wrigley Field as the Astros beat the Cubs 10-3 on April 21. He connected for a solo shot in the first and a three-run blast in the third, both off Scott Sanders, and then a two-run homer in the seventh against Rodney Myers. Bagwell's three long balls gave him 225 homers with Houston, breaking Jimmy Wynn's franchise record of 223. On June 9, the Astros wrapped up a three-game interleague series with the Chicago White Sox at Comiskey Park by whipping the Sox 13-4. Bagwell started the game 0 for 3 but then equaled his career high of six RBIs again by connecting for a three-run homer against Sean Lowe in the sixth, a solo shot against Bill Simas in the eighth, and a two-run home run against Keith Foulke in the ninth.

Darrin Jackson hit four grand slams in his career, each coming with a different team. Jackson hammered his first career slam with San Diego against Chicago's Bob Scanlan in the sixth inning at Wrigley Field on August 25, 1991. In the first inning of the game on June 7, 1994, Jackson hit his next slam for the White Sox against Toronto's Pat Hentgen at Comiskey Park. Following a couple of years in the Japanese League, Jackson returned to the majors in 1997 with the Minnesota Twins and smacked a grand slam against Toby Borland at the Metrodome in the fourth inning on May 16. His last grand slam was with the Milwaukee Brewers on July 28, 1998, when he connected against St. Louis pitcher Rich Croushore at Busch Stadium. Jackson retired at the end of the 1999 season with 80 career homers.

Hank Aaron smashed 40 homers for the Atlanta Braves in 1973 and finished the year with a career total of 713, one behind Babe Ruth's record. That season Aaron had the fewest hits (118), fewest extra-base hits (53), and fewest total bases (252) for a player with a 40-homer season.

On September 7, 1998, Mark McGwire hammered his 61st homer of the season against Cubs' pitcher Mike Morgan – *on his father's 61st birthday*. The blast tied Roger Maris' 37-year-old, single-season home run record and was McGwire's 210th homer since the beginning of the 1995 season, breaking Babe Ruth's record of 209 homers during a four-year span. The next day, McGwire broke Maris' record with a line drive shot that just cleared the left field wall against Steve Trachsel. The homer was measured at 341 feet, which turned out to be the shortest home run of the year.

Jimmy Piersall celebrated his 100th career home run by rounding the bases in an unusual fashion. Piersall connected in the fifth inning on June 23, 1963, at the Polo Grounds and then, much to the displeasure of Philadelphia's Dallas Green who had given up the homer, turned his back to the plate and began his trip around the bases facing backwards. A rule was soon implemented that outlawed this practice. Piersall's 100th homer was the only National League homer among his 104 career round-trippers.

Only once in major league history has a team hit ten home runs in a single game. On September 14, 1987, Toronto pounded Baltimore 18-3 at Exhibition Stadium. The Blue Jays hammered ten long balls, including three by catcher Ernie Whitt and two each from Rance Mulliniks and George Bell. Lloyd Moseby and rookies Fred McGriff and Rob Ducey each slugged one. Ducey's home run was the first of his career and the only one managed in 48 at-bats in 1987. With the game out of hand, Baltimore's Cal Ripken was replaced at shortstop in the bottom of the eighth, ending his streak of 8,243 consecutive innings played.

On May 26, 1997, the Cubs beat the Pirates 2-1 with two of the runs resulting from inside-the park home runs *in the same inning.* In the top of the sixth inning at Three Rivers Stadium with the Cubs already up 1-0, Sammy Sosa circled the bases and slid safely into home when two Pirate outfielders collided near the wall in right-center and the ball rolled into the right field corner. In the home half of the inning, Pittsburgh's speedy second baseman Tony Womack scored the Pirates' only run by racing around the bases after center fielder Doug Glanville dove for his line drive and allowed the ball to roll all the way to the wall.

Rafael Belliard went 1,869 at-bats – *and over ten years* – between his two career home runs. The light-hitting shortstop clubbed a three-run homer on May 5, 1987, against San Diego's Eric Show at Jack Murphy Stadium. His next homer was not until September 26, 1997, when he took New York Met pitcher Brian Bohanon deep at Shea Stadium for a two-run shot. Belliard's unlikely home run helped the Braves beat the Mets 7-6 in 11 innings and accounted for two of his three RBIs in 1997.

Only seven times has a player hit 40 homers while striking out 40 times or less – *but Cincinnati Red slugger Ted Kluszewski did it three straight years.* Kluszewski hit 40 long balls while fanning just 34 times in 1953 and then smacked 49 homers with only 35 strikeouts the following season. In 1955 he powered 47 homers while whiffing 40 times. The next season Kluszewski's strikeout total was still only 31, but his home run total fell to 35. For his career, Big Klu hit 279 homers and struck out only 365 times.

Johnny Mize, Carl Yastrzemski and Jay Buhner each topped the 40-home run mark in three different seasons – *but never hit 30 homers in any other season*. Mize belted 43 in 1940, 51 in 1947, and 40 in 1948, with his next best year being 1939 when he hit 28 homers. Yaz hit 44 homers during his 1967 Triple Crown season and hit 40 in both 1969 and 1970. His next highest total of 28 homers came in 1977. Buhner posted totals of 40, 44, and 40 homers for the Seattle Mariners from 1995 to 1997. His next best seasons were 1991 and 1993 when he hit 27 home runs each season.

The 1979 Houston Astros are the last team to hit fewer than 50 home runs in a full season. The Astros finished with 49 homers, 25 fewer than the New York Mets, the team with the next fewest. Jose Cruz led the Astros with nine, Terry Puhl had eight, and Enos Cabell, Art Howe and Cesar Cedeno chipped in six each. Despite their lack of power, Houston compiled a record of 89-73 and finished just 1 1/2 games behind Cincinnati in the National League West race.

Mel Ott led the New York Giants in home runs for 18 consecutive seasons from 1928 to 1945. During this span, Ott's lowest total was 18 in both 1928 and 1943 and his best year was 1929 when he hit 42 homers. In 1936 Ott hit 33 homers and the next highest total on the team was only nine by both Hank Leiber and Gus Mancuso. Seven times during his reign as Giant home run champ Ott at least *doubled* the output of his closest teammate.

Texas pitcher Bobby Witt hit the first home run by an American League pitcher since the introduction of the designated hitter in 1973 when he connected for a solo shot against Dodger hurler Ismael Valdes leading off the sixth inning at Dodger Stadium on June 30, 1997. Prior to Witt's homer, the last AL pitcher to go deep was

Roric Harrison of Baltimore who connected against Cleveland on October 3, 1972.

In just his seventh major league at-bat, Houston rookie pitcher Butch Henry collected an inside-the-park three-run homer – *for his first major league hit* – against Pittsburgh's Doug Drabek in the second inning at Three Rivers Stadium on May 8, 1992. Despite his homer, Henry pitched only two innings (giving up three hits and two earned runs) as Pittsburgh downed the Astros 6-3. It was Henry's only career home run in 151 at-bats.

In his first major league at-bat on April 23, 1952, knuckleball pitcher Hoyt Wilhelm homered into the lower right field stands at the Polo Grounds against Dick Hoover of the Boston Braves – *the only home run he would hit in 432 career at-bats*. Pitching 5.1 innings of middle relief, Wilhelm gave up six hits and two runs and was rewarded with his first big league win. On June 4, 1953, in his 12th at-bat of the year (and 50th of his career) Wilhelm hit his first career triple to break a 3-3 seventh-inning tie with the Reds and got the victory when the Giants blew the game open with seven more runs in the eighth. Although he would bat another 384 times before retiring in 1972, Wilhelm would never hit another triple.

Bernie Williams and Jorge Posada are the only teammates to homer from each side of the plate in the same game. Williams homered from the left side against Frank Castillo in the first inning, Posada did the same in the second, and then they each homered from the right side off Clayton Andrews in the fourth during the Yank's 10-7 win at Toronto on April 23, 2000.

Roberto Clemente rallied the Pirates past the Cubs 9-8 on July 25, 1956, by blasting an inside-the-park grand slam in the bottom of the ninth inning at Forbes Field. The Cubs had scored seven in the eighth to overcome a four-run Pittsburgh lead and added one in the ninth to make it 8-5, but the Pirates rallied with two walks and a single, bringing Clemente to the plate as the winning run. Chicago brought in Jim Brosnan in relief of Turk Lown and Clemente jumped on his first pitch, sending it to deep left-center field, clearing the bases and tying the game. Pirates' manager Bobby Bragan attempted to hold Clemente at third with no one out, but Clemente ran through Bragan's "stop sign" and slid safely into home, just beating a close play at the plate. Clemente is the *only* player to end a game with an inside-the-park grand slam.

Willie Mays is one of only nine players to have two 50-homer seasons, but his seasons were unique in that they came an entire decade apart – he belted 51 homers for the 1955 New York Giants and 52 for the 1965 San Francisco Giants.

After last appearing in the major leagues in 1937, Babe Herman returned in 1945 due to the shortage of players caused by World War II. Herman got nine hits in 34 at-bats with the Brooklyn Dodgers, including a homer against Ken Gables at Forbes Field on July 15. The blast was Herman's first big league homer since he connected against Cardinals' pitcher Roy Parmelee at Sportsman's Park on September 24, 1936, as a member of the Cincinnati Reds. Herman's 1945 homer was also his first for Brooklyn since September 18, 1931, when he clouted one against Charlie Root at Wrigley Field. The span of 5,049 days between Herman's Dodger home runs remains the record for the largest gap between home runs with one team.

On April 21, 2000, the Anaheim Angels produced the first trio of players to each homer in the same two innings of a game. The Angels beat Tampa Bay 9-6 as Mo Vaughn, Tim Salmon, and Troy Glaus each homered off Dwight Gooden in the fourth inning and Roberto Hernandez in the ninth.

In 1995 San Diego's Ken Caminiti became the first switch hitter to homer from each side of the plate in a game three times in one season – *and he did it within a four-game span.* On September 16 in the second game of a six-game homestand, Caminiti homered lefthanded in the first inning against Chicago's Steve Trachsel and righthanded in the seventh against Larry Casian. The next night Caminiti continued his assault on the Cubs' pitching staff by connecting from the right side against Roberto Rivera in the fifth and from the left side against Turk Wendell in the seventh. He joined

Eddie Murray (May 8 and 9, 1987) as the only player to accomplish the feat in back-to-back games. Following a hitless game against Colorado, Caminiti came back on September 19 against the Rockies to homer lefty against Armando Reynoso in the second and righty against Bryan Hickerson in the seventh. The next season Caminiti would break his own record. On the way to a .326 average, 40 homers, 130 RBIs and a unanimous MVP Award, he homered from each side of the plate in *four* games –August 1, August 21, August 28 (12 innings), and September 11.

On April 19, 1977, Brooks Robinson hit a dramatic three-run, pinch-hit home run against Cleveland's Dave LaRoche with one out in the bottom of the 10th to bring the Orioles from behind to defeat the Indians 6-5. It was the last of Robinson's 268 career homers and was the *only* time he connected in 31 at-bats as a pinch hitter.

Bill Buckner's last home run was against Kirk McCaskill on April 25, 1990, at Fenway Park – *and was the only inside-the-parker among his 174 career homers.* Despite his infamous bad legs, the 40-year-old Buckner circled the bases in the fourth inning when Angels' outfielder Claudell Washington fell into the bullpen behind the short right field wall while attempting to catch Buckner's drive to deep right. Buckner's previous home run had also come against McCaskill back on June 3, 1989, at Anaheim Stadium.

Injuries limited Mark McGwire to only 423 at-bats in 1996, yet he still managed to hit 52 home runs, making him the player with the fewest at-bats to have a 50-homer season. He broke Babe Ruth's 1920 record of 54 homers in 458 at-bats.

Ted Williams owns a share of the record of homering in four consecutive at-bats – *doing it over a span of five games.* Suffering from a bad chest cold, Williams struck out as a pinch hitter on September 1, 1957, and was then out of the lineup until he pinch-hit again on September 17 and hit a solo homer against A's pitcher Tom Morgan. Following a walk as a pinch hitter on September 18, Williams made his third consecutive pinch-hitting appearance on September 20 and homered in the ninth against Whitey Ford at Yankee Stadium.

Williams returned to the starting lineup the next day and hit a grand slam in the second inning against Bob Turley and then walked the next three times up, *each time on four pitches.* The next day, September 22, he walked in the first inning before homering against Tom Sturdivant in the fourth. Williams' home run streak ended in the sixth inning when he singled.

No player has ever hit more homers in a season than his team won games. The smallest difference is four, achieved by Wally Berger in 1935 and Sammy Sosa in 1999. Berger hit 34 homers for a terrible Boston Brave team that finished with a record of 38-115. He accounted for 45.3 percent of Boston's 75 homers and finished well ahead of the six homers by second-place Babe Ruth who appeared in 28 games for Boston following the end of his Yankees' career. Sosa hit 63 long balls, a full 37 more than his closest teammate Henry Rodriguez, but his Chicago Cubs ended the season 67-95.

Dave Kingman homered for teams in each of the four divisions in 1977. Kingman started the season in the NL East with the New York Mets and homered nine times in 58 games. After being traded to the San Diego Padres of the NL West and swatting 11 homers in 56 games, he was placed him on waivers by the Padres. Kingman was claimed by California of the AL West and smacked two homers in ten games for the Angels before being sold to the Yankees, ending the season back in New York and hitting four homers in eight games for the Yankees in the AL East.

Mark McGwire hit 16th-inning, game-winning home runs *in consecutive games.* On July 3, 1988, McGwire homered against John Cerutti in the top of the 16th at Exhibition Stadium as the A's beat the Blue Jays 9-8. The next day at Cleveland's Municipal Stadium, McGwire hit a solo homer against Brad Havens to break a 2-2 tie in the top of the 16th and propelled the A's to a 4-2 win over Cleveland. McGwire's other nine career extra-inning homers were in the 10th inning (seven), 11th (one) and 12th (one).

Pete Rose hit the last two of his 160 homers at Wrigley Field in 1985 after not hitting a homer in over two years. Rose homered to lead off the fourth inning against Chicago's Scott Sanderson on May 20. The home run was his first since September 18, 1982, and the run he scored as a result tied Hank Aaron's National League record of 2,107 runs scored. Rose's final round-tripper was a two-run shot at Wrigley Field against Derek Botelho in the second inning on September 6. The homer was his 4,188th hit, pulling Rose to within three hits of Ty Cobb's all-time record.

Among the players with 500 or more home runs, Mark McGwire is seventh with 583 home runs but ranks *last* in games (1,874), hits (1,626), doubles (252), triples (6), RBIs (1,414), total bases (3,639), runs (1,167), stolen bases (12), and extra-base hits (841).

Tony Gwynn had just three grand slams and just two inside-the-park home runs but got one of each with a single swing of the bat on June 26, 1997. The Padres' star recorded an inside-the-park grand slam when Dodgers' left fielder Brett Butler injured his shoulder while making a futile diving attempt of Gwynn's seventh inning line drive off Mark Guthrie. Gwynn's hit broke a 4-4 tie and carried the Padres to 9-7 win.

Sammy Sosa produced three of the eight 60-homer seasons in major league history – *but did not lead the league in any of those years*. Sosa belted 66 home runs in 1998 and finished behind Mark McGwire's 70 and then hit 63 more four-baggers in 1999 but again was second to McGwire who hit 65. In 2001 Sosa smashed 64 long balls only to finish behind Barry Bonds' record 73 homers. Sosa did lead the National League with 50 homers in 2000 and 49 homers in 2002.

Fred McGriff's last home run was at San Diego's new Petco Park on June 17, 2004, when he connected in the sixth against Adam Eaton, pulling the ball down the right field line. Petco Park was the 43rd different ballpark in which he hit a homer – breaking a tie with Ellis Burks – and was also his 493rd homer, tying him with Lou Gehrig on the all-time list. The Devil Rays' next series was at Arizona's Bank One Ballpark, a park where McGriff had never homered. McGriff appeared in the game on June 20 but went 0 for 3.

After hitting just .181 with two homers and seven RBIs in 27 games, McGriff was designated for assignment by the Devil Rays on July 17. He ended his stay in Tampa Bay with 99 homers in a Devil Ray uniform – just short of joining Reggie Jackson and Darrell Evans as the only players to hit 100 homers with three different teams.

On May 15, 1989, Bob Dernier hit a three-run homer – *his only one of the season, the last of his 23 career home runs, and his only career inside-the-park homer* - in the bottom of the twelfth to beat the Giants 3-2 at Veterans Stadium. San Francisco's Scott Garrelts and Don Carman hooked up in a pitcher's duel, each pitching nine scoreless innings. Dernier entered the game in the 10th and kept the game scoreless by throwing Will Clark out at home to kill a Giants' rally. San Francisco finally put runs on the board in the top of the twelfth when Clark and Kevin Mitchell each hit a solo homer against Steve Bedrosian. Dernier came to the plate in the bottom of the inning with Dickie Thon and Steve Lake on base and two men out. He hooked a 1-1 pitch from Craig Lefferts into the left field corner where the ball took a crazy carom and rolled along the base of the wall toward center field. Mitchell finally chased it down, but his throw was off-line and allowed Dernier to slide safely into home.

Mark McGwire homered into the second deck of Seattle's Kingdome *twice in one inning.* During Oakland's 13-11 win over Seattle on September 22, 1996, McGwire led off the fifth inning with his 51st home run of the year against Rusty Meacham. The A's batted around, and later in the inning he blasted his last home run of the 1996 season, a grand slam against rookie Matt Wagner. McGwire's blasts were estimated at 473 and 481 feet.

Ralph Garr hit two extra-inning home runs among his 75 career homers – *and they came in the same game.* On May 17, 1971, the Mets had a 3-2 lead over Atlanta heading in the bottom of the 10th due to a Donn Clendenon homer in the top of the inning. Mets' starter Tom Seaver retired the first two Braves and was just one out away from a victory when Garr tied the game with a solo blast. The game remained tied until the bottom of the 12th when Garr ended it with a solo homer against reliever Ron Taylor. Garr's heroics make him just one of five players to hit two extra-inning homers in one game – but the only to never hit another homer after the ninth inning.

Entering the Cub-Diamondback game on July 27, 1998, Sammy Sosa had 246 home runs but no grand slams – *the most homers ever by a player without one* – and then connected with the bases loaded in back-to-back games. Sosa blasted his first career slam off Arizona's Alan Embree in the eighth inning at Bank One Ballpark. The next night he victimized the Diamondbacks again when he launched another one in the fifth inning against Bob Wolcott.

Only three sluggers have hit 200 home runs in each league – Frank Robinson (343 in the NL, 243 in the AL), Mark McGwire (220, 363) and Fred McGriff (269, 224).

League Leaders

Ty Cobb, Ted Williams, and Tony Gwynn each won two batting titles with a season average *below their career average.* Cobb finished his career with a major league record batting average of .366 and won ten American League batting titles, including titles in 1907 when he hit .350 and in 1908 when he finished at .324. Williams captured seven AL batting championships, including batting crowns in 1947 when he batted .343 and in 1958 when he hit .328 – both below his lifetime mark of .344. Gwynn ended his career with eight National League batting crowns and a lifetime average of .338. Two of his batting titles were in 1988 when he led the NL with a .313 average and in 1989 when he batted .336.

In his 12-year career, injury-plagued outfielder Lenny Dykstra had only two seasons in which he collected more than 127 hits – *but he led the league each of those years.* Dykstra topped the NL in hits with the Phillies in 1990 with 192 hits and again in 1993 with 194 hits.

On April 17, 1960, Detroit and Cleveland announced a blockbuster trade in which the American League's defending home run champ was traded straight-up for the American League's defending batting champ. Harvey Kuenn, who led the AL with a .353 average in 1959, was sent to Cleveland for Rocky Colavito, whose 42 homers in 1959 tied with Harmon Killebrew for the AL title. In the 1960 season, Kuenn lead the Indians with a .308 average and finished fifth in the AL batting race, while Colavito topped the Tigers with 35 homers to finish fourth in the league.

The 1993 Toronto Blue Jays are the only team since 1900 to produce the top three hitters in the league. John Olerud led the league with a .363 average, followed by Paul Molitor at .332, and by Roberto Alomar who batted .326. The trio's hot hitting led the Blue Jays to a second consecutive World Series title.

George Brett is the only player to win batting titles in three decades. The Kansas City Royals' superstar led the American League in hitting in 1976 (.333), 1980 (.390), and 1990 (.329).

Boston Red Sox Johnny Pesky had three 200-hit seasons and each time it was good enough to lead the American League. Pesky led the AL in hits each of the first three years of his career. He started with 205 hits in 1942 and, after missing two seasons to World War II, posted league-leading totals of 208 hits in 1946 and 207 in 1947. Another Red Sox player wasn't quite so lucky – Wade Boggs had seven consecutive 200-hit seasons (1983-1989) but led the American League *only once*. He paced the league with 240 hits in 1985 and finished second in 1983, 1984, 1988, and tied for second in 1989.

Despite 504 home runs and 1,917 RBIs, the only year that Eddie Murray led the league in either category was during the strike-shortened 1981 season. Murray played in 99 games and finished in a four-way tie for the American League lead with 22 homers and knocked in a league-leading 78 runs. Although it was good enough to lead the AL, his 78 RBIs was the lowest total Murray would have during his first 17 seasons.

Duane Ward of the Toronto Blue Jays tied for the American League lead with 45 saves in 1993 – *and then never recorded another save*. Ward missed the entire 1994 season with a partially torn rotator cuff, pitched only 2.2 innings in 1995, and then never pitched again.

Despite hitting .300 only six times and a lifetime batting average of just .285, Carl Yastrzemski won three AL batting titles. Yaz paced the AL in 1963 with a .321 average and led the Red Sox to the 1967 World Series by winning the Triple Crown, which included an average of .326. In the 1968 season, Yastrzemski was the only American League regular to hit .300 when he led the league with a .301 average, the lowest average ever to win a batting crown.

Ted Williams led the American League in walks for six consecutive seasons in which he played. Williams topped the league in 1941 and 1942 and, following a three-year stint in World War II, led the AL again each year from 1946 to 1949. Despite a .344 lifetime batting average and 2,654 career hits, Williams' ability to draw walks kept him from having a 200-hit season or leading the league in hits. His highest hit total was in 1949 when he banged out 194 hits and finished second in the league, nine hits behind Dale Mitchell.

Toronto teammates Roger Clemens and Pat Hentgen tied for the American League lead in three categories in 1997 – they each pitched 264 innings, including nine complete games and three shutouts. However, the similarities ended there because Clemens was 21-7 and led the league in strikeouts (292) and ERA (2.05) while winning the Cy Young Award. Hentgen finished 15-10 with 160 whiffs and a 3.68 ERA. Despite pitching the same number of innings, Hentgen allowed 31 homers, compared to only nine by Clemens.

As part of his record streak of 2,632 consecutive games, Cal Ripken, Jr. was in the lineup every day from the opening of the 1990 season until September 20, 1998 – *and still finished fifth in games played in the 1990s.* During the 1999 season, back injuries forced the Baltimore ironman to the disabled list for the first time in his career, limiting him to just 86 games. Ripken finished the decade with 1,475 games played, trailing Rafael Palmeiro, Craig Biggio, Mark Grace, and Jay Bell.

In 1948 St. Louis's Stan Musial led the National League in *nine* major offensive categories but did not claim the NL's Triple Crown because the one category that he did not win was home runs. Musial topped the NL with a .376 average, 230 hits, 46 doubles, 18 triples, 131 RBIs, 135 runs, 429 total bases, a .450 on-base percentage, and a .702 slugging percentage. He did hit a career-high 39 homers yet finished behind the 40 homers of New York's Johnny Mize and

Pittsburgh's Ralph Kiner. Musial would finish with 475 career home runs but never lead the league in homers.

Paul Molitor led the AL in hits three times – *each time with a different club*. Molitor paced the AL with 216 hits for the 1991 Milwaukee Brewers, with 211 hits for the 1993 Toronto Blue Jays, and with 225 hits for the 1996 Minnesota Twins.

Hoyt Wilhelm pitched enough innings to qualify for the ERA title only twice in his 21-year career – *and both times he led the league*. As a rookie in 1952 with the New York Giants, Wilhelm did not start a single game but still managed enough innings to lead the National League with an ERA of 2.43 because he appeared in 71 games, compiling a 15-3 record in 159.1 innings. Wilhelm also led the American League in ERA in 1959 when he made 27 of his 52 career starts. He threw 226 innings for the Baltimore Orioles but was just 15-11 despite posting a 2.19 ERA.

Fred McGriff is the last player to win both the NL and the AL home run crown with fewer than 40 homers. He led the American League when he hit 36 for the 1989 Blue Jays and topped the National League with 35 for the Padres in 1992.

Pittsburgh's Ralph Kiner led the National League in home runs his first seven years in the major leagues. After edging Johnny Mize (23 to 22) to win his first home run title in 1946, the Pirate slugger exploded in his second season with 51 homers to tie Mize for the NL crown. Kiner belted 40 round-trippers in 1948 to once again tie with Mize and then popped a career-best 54 homers in 1949 to beat Stan Musial by 18 homers, tying the second largest margin in NL history. Kiner led the league outright in 1950 and in 1951 before tying for the NL lead again in 1952, this time with Hank Sauer's 37 homers. Kiner's 294 homers in his seven league-leading seasons accounted for almost 80 percent of his 369 career home runs.

Chuck Klein is one of only seven hitters to get 250 or more hits in a season – *but he is the only one who did not lead his league*. Klein banged out 250 hits for the Philadelphia Phillies in 1930 and still trailed New York Giant Bill Terry who led the National League – and tied Lefty O'Doul's NL record set just one season earlier – by smacking 254 hits.

In the 1907 season, Ty Cobb and Honus Wagner were the AL and NL batting champs, and each batted .350. It was 93 seasons later before the NL and AL batting champions would again have the same average – *but then happened in back-to-back years*. In the 2000 season Nomar Garciaparra and Todd Helton each hit .372 to claim the AL and NL batting crowns. The second-place batters in the 2000 season, Darin Erstad in the AL and Moises Alou in the NL, tied as well with averages of .355. The following season Ichiro Suzuki topped the AL and Larry Walker led the NL, each with an average of .350.

In each season from 2001 to 2003, the Arizona Diamondbacks' pitching staff, led by Randy Johnson and Curt Schilling, struck out more batters in a single season than all but four pitching staffs in big league history – *but they did not lead the National League in any of those years*. The top four strikeouts pitching staffs of all time belong to the Chicago Cubs, who did it from 2001 to 2004. The Cubs edged the Diamondbacks in strikeouts in 2001 (1,344 to 1,297), 2002 (1,333 to 1,303) and 2003 (1,404 to 1,291). The 2004 Chicago staff struck out 1,346 batters while Arizona (minus Schilling who went to Boston) dropped to third in the NL with 1,153. Chicago's hitters led the league by fanning 1,269 times in 2002, making the 2002 Cubs the only squad to lead the league in both batting strikeouts and pitching strikeouts in the same season.

Nolan Ryan of the Houston Astros led the National League in 1987 with 270 strikeouts and an ERA of 2.76 – *but finished with a record of 8-16*. Ryan's tough-luck season ended his streak of 16 consecutive seasons with at least ten victories and, since he reached double-figure win totals each year from 1988 to 1991, kept him from having 21 straight seasons of ten or more wins – *which would have broken Cy Young's record by two seasons*. Ryan also holds the dubious distinction of being the only pitcher to strike out 300 batters in a season and finish with a losing record. He struck out 327 batters for the California Angels in 1976 and posted a 3.36 ERA, but he still finished 17-18.

In the 2004 season when he shattered his own single-season record by drawing 232 walks, Barry Bonds had more *intentional* walks than the American League leader had *total* walks. Bonds had 120 intentional walks while Eric Chavez led the AL with just 95 total walks.

Ron Santo managed to lead the NL in walks four times (1964 and 1966-1968) despite never having a 100-walk season. Santo's walk totals for those years were 86, 95, 96 and 96.

George Earnshaw finished second in the AL in strikeouts for three consecutive years – *yet did not lead his own team in strikeouts once*. Earnshaw finished behind his teammate Lefty Grove in 1929 (170 to 149), 1930 (209 to 193), and 1931 (175 to 152).

In his nine-year major league career, Phil Douglas led the National League once in winning percentage (.733 with a record of 11-4) and ERA (2.63) – *both in his last season in the majors*. Shortly after giving up five runs in the Giants' 7-0 loss to Pittsburgh on July 30, 1922, the alcoholic Douglas was fined and suspended by his manager John McGraw. In a drunken state, Douglas wrote a letter to a former teammate, now in St. Louis, offering to disappear from the team (for a price) rather than help McGraw win the NL pennant. The letter eventually wound up in the hands of Commissioner Kenesaw Mountain Landis who banned Douglas from baseball for life.

Phil Niekro won 318 games, leading the league in wins twice – *and also leading the league in losses four straight years*. Niekro tied for the lead with 20 losses in 1977 and then led outright with totals of 18, 20, and 18 over the next three years. The only other 300-game winner to lead his league in losses more than once is Steve Carlton, who did it in 1970 and 1973. In the 1979 season, Niekro posted a 3.39 ERA in 342 innings and threw 23 complete games, not only leading the league with 20 losses but also winning a NL-best 21 games – making him the *only* pitcher to top the league in each category in the same season.

Mike Marshall holds the record for most appearances by a pitcher in a season – *in each league.* Marshall appeared in a major league record 106 games for the 1974 Los Angeles Dodgers and set the American League record by pitching in 90 games for the 1979 Minnesota Twins.

Bill Madlock won four batting crowns but is not in the Hall of Fame. Madlock led the National League in hitting with the Chicago Cubs in 1975 (.354) and 1976 (.339) and with the Pittsburgh Pirates in 1981 (.341) and 1983 (.323). He finished with a .305 career average.

Yankees' legend Mickey Mantle led the AL in homers four times – *but only drove in 100 runs in one of those years.* The only one of his league-leading home run seasons in which Mantle topped 100-RBI mark was in 1956 when he won the Triple Crown with 52 homers, 130 RBIs and a .353 average. His other home run titles came in 1955, 1958, and 1960 when he had RBI totals of 99, 97, and 94. Mantle is the only player since 1920 to win three home run crowns while driving in fewer than 100 runs.

Managers

The 1977 Texas Rangers had four managers – *within an 11-game span*. Frank Lucchesi began the season as the team's skipper but was dismissed on June 21 with the team struggling to a 31-31 record. Eddie Stanky, who had not managed since 1968 with the White Sox, took over and won his first game at Minnesota the following night. After the game, the 60-year-old Stanky resigned after having second thoughts about managing again and the Rangers named Connie Ryan as the interim manager. Ryan guided the team to a 2-4 record until Billy Hunter was named the permanent skipper on June 28. The squad responded to Hunter's hiring by going 60-33 over the rest of the season and finishing second in the AL West with a record of 94-68.

Gene Mauch managed for 26 years – winning 1,902 big league games – but never won a pennant. Mauch did come excruciatingly close to the World Series three times. In 1964 his Phillies' squad had a 6 1/2 game lead in the NL with just two weeks left in the season but then lost ten straight to finish one game back of St. Louis. His 1982 California Angels won the AL West with a 93-69 record and took the first two games of the ALCS against Milwaukee. The two teams resumed the best-of-five series in Milwaukee, and the Brewers won three straight games to steal the pennant. In 1986 Mauch's Angels managed to come even closer than they did in 1982 and still not win the AL pennant. The Angels opened the ALCS, now a best-of-seven format, by winning three of the first four against Boston. Mauch and his crew entered the top of the ninth of Game 5 with 5-2 lead, just three outs from the World Series. Don Baylor hit a two-run homer to close the gap and later, with the Angels just one strike away from victory, Dave Henderson hit a two-run homer against Donnie Moore to give Boston the lead. The Angels rallied to tie it in the bottom of the ninth, but Boston won in the 11th and then won the ALCS by taking Games 6 and 7 back in Boston. In addition to managing four teams (Phillies, Expos, Twins, and Angels) that never reached a World Series, Mauch played for six different teams (Dodgers, Pirates, Cubs, Braves, Cardinals, and Red Sox) from 1944 to 1957, none of which reached the Series.

Sparky Anderson is the only manager to lead a team from each league to a World Series title. Anderson piloted the Cincinnati Reds to NL pennants in 1970, 1972, 1975, and 1976, winning the World Series over Boston in 1975 and New York in 1976. Anderson took over as Detroit's skipper in 1979 and led the Tigers to the 1984 pennant and a World Series victory over San Diego.

Frank Robinson was baseball's first black manager – *in both the National and American League*. Robinson was the player-manager of the Cleveland Indians in 1975 and hit an opening-day, solo homer in his first at-bat as their skipper on April 8. He remained at the helm of the Indians through the first 57 games of the 1977 season. In the strike-plagued 1981 season, Robinson was hired to manage the San Francisco Giants in the NL and stayed with them through the first 106 games of the 1984 campaign.

The Boston Red Sox were managed by two men while winning a record 24 consecutive home games in 1988. With Boston floundering at the All-Star break with a 43-42 record, manager John McNamara was dismissed and replaced with Joe Morgan. The Red Sox responded by winning 19 of the next 20, with the only loss coming at Texas by the score of 9-8. Before the managerial change, the Red Sox had won their last five games at Fenway Park under Morgan, and they stayed hot by winning their next 19 at home before Detroit hammered Roger Clemens and beat them 18-6 on August 14. The second-half surge lifted Boston from nine games out at the All-Star break and propelled them to the AL East title.

Joe Torre is undefeated in six games as an All-Star manager. Torre guided the American League to wins in 1996, 1999, 2000, 2001, and 2004. He was also the AL skipper in the 2002 game that ended in a 7-7 tie.

Only two managers have led three different teams to the World Series. Bill McKechnie won pennants with Pittsburgh in 1925, St. Louis in 1928, and Cincinnati in 1939 and 1940. His teams were 2-2 in World Series play, winning in 1925 and 1940. Dick Williams' record was also 2-2 in the World Series. He led Boston (1967), Oakland (1972 and 1973) and San Diego (1984) to World Series appearances, winning both times with Oakland.

Al Lopez managed the only two American League teams that beat the New York Yankees for the AL pennant between 1949 and 1964. During the Yankees' string of 14 AL pennants in 16 years, Lopez guided the 1954 Cleveland Indians to the World Series by winning 111 games – an AL record that stood until 1998. Although they finished second to Cleveland in 1954, New York did win 103 games, their highest total during their remarkable 16-year run. In 1959 Lopez and the Chicago White Sox won the pennant with 94 wins, five games ahead of Cleveland and 15 games in front of the Yankees.

Milestones

Pete Rose broke Max Carey's National League record by recording his 10th career five-hit game *during his final week as an active player*. On August 11, 1986, the Cincinnati Reds player-manager inserted himself into the starting lineup for the first time since August 2 and went 5 for 5 with four singles and a double and drove in three runs against the San Francisco Giants at Riverfront Stadium. The five hits were his first since July 30 and raised his average from .204 to .222. Following a couple of failed pinch-hit attempts, Rose started himself again on August 14 against the Giants and collected the last three hits and last RBI of his career. During an August 15 doubleheader, Rose went 0 for 1 as a pinch hitter in the first game and 0 for 4 as a starter in the second contest. The next day Rose was 0 for 4 at the plate against the San Diego Padres before ending his major league career on August 17 by striking out as a pinch hitter against Goose Gossage.

Hank Aaron, Willie Mays, Eddie Murray, and Rafael Palmeiro are the only four players to accumulate at least 3,000 hits and 500 home runs. Murray is the only one of the group who did it without the benefit of a 200-hit or a 35-homer season. His career-high in hits was 186 hits in 1980, and his best home run season was 33 in 1983.

Paul Molitor knocked out his 3,000th career hit with a triple on September 16, 1996, against Kansas City Royals' pitcher Jose Rosado – making him the only player to reach the 3,000-hit mark with a three-bagger. Molitor finished the year with a league-high 225 hits, becoming the only player to top the league in hits or to have a 200-hit season in the same year as his 3,000th hit.

St. Louis Cardinals' speedster Lou Brock set two stolen base records in one game. On September 10, 1974, Brock's first-inning steal of second base against the Phillies tied Maury Wills' 1962 record of 104 steals in a season and was also Brock's 739th career theft – breaking Max Carey's NL record of 738. In the seventh inning, Brock would steal second again to pass Wills and set a new single-season record. Brock finished 1974 with 118 steals, a mark that would last until Rickey Henderson swiped 130 bases in 1982.

Just prior to his tragic death in a plane crash on December 31, 1972, Pittsburgh's Roberto Clemente became the 11th player to reach 3,000 hits. In the last regular season at-bat of his career, Clemente got his milestone hit when he led off the fourth inning with a double against New York's Jon Matlack at Three Rivers Stadium on September 30. Although he never batted again, Clemente appeared in one more game on October 3 to tie Honus Wagner's team record of 2,433 games played.

In the 1985 season, Rod Carew got his 3,000th hit and Tom Seaver won his 300th game – *on the same day*. On August 4 at Yankee Stadium, Seaver struck out seven and gave up only six singles as he pitched a complete game against New York for his 300th career win. Later in the day and across the country in California, Carew singled to left in the third inning against Minnesota's Frank Viola for his 3,000th career hit.

In an unprecedented stretch in major league history, major career milestones were reached on *three consecutive days*. On August 5, 1999, Mark McGwire hit a solo home run against San Diego's Andy Ashby in the third inning at Busch Stadium, making him just the 16th player to hit 500 homers. In the eighth, McGwire took Ashby deep again for his 501st home run. Tony Gwynn entered the game with 2,998 career hits but could only manage a ninth-inning double, just missing reaching the 3,000-hit mark in the same game as McGwire's milestone homer. The next night in Montreal, Gwynn singled in the first against rookie Dan Smith to become the 22nd player to achieve 3,000 hits. With the pressure off, Gwynn then slapped three more hits to finish the night 4 for 5. Gwynn's 3,000th hit came on August 6, which was his mother's 64th birthday and the sixth anniversary of his 2,000th hit. The following night, August 7, Tampa Bay's Wade Boggs joined Gwynn in the 3,000-hit club. Entering the game needing three hits, Boggs grounded out to second in the first and then collected RBI singles against Cleveland's Charles Nagy in his next two at-bats before lining a pitch from reliever Chris Haney over the right field wall in the sixth for a two-run homer. The homer was just his second of the season – as well as the 118th and last of his career – and made him the only player to hit a home run for his 3,000th hit.

Pete Rose and Willie Davis each got their 2,000th hit on June 19, 1973. Davis' 2,000th was two-run home run in the sixth inning against Atlanta's Phil Niekro at Dodger Stadium. Up the coast in San Francisco, Rose went 4 for 5 against the Giants, including a sixth-inning single against Ron Bryant for his 2,000th career hit. Rose would collect another 2,256 hits, but Davis would finish his career with a total of 2,561.

In the at-bat *before* he broke Babe Ruth's career home run record, Hank Aaron topped Willie Mays' National League record for runs scored. Aaron entered the 1974 season with 2,060 runs scored, two runs behind Mays. On April 4 at Cincinnati, Aaron tied Ruth by hitting homer his 714th homer and also scored two runs to pull even with Mays. Four days later at Atlanta, Aaron walked in the second and scored on a double by Dusty Baker to pass Mays and then hit his historic homer in the fourth inning to pass Ruth.

With one swing of the bat, Carlton Fisk set both a major league record and a White Sox team record. In the second inning of the second game of a doubleheader against Texas on August 17, 1990, Fisk homered against Charlie Hough at Arlington Stadium. The homer was his 328th home run as a catcher, breaking the mark set by Johnny Bench, and was also his 187th homer as a member of the

White Sox, breaking Harold Baines' club record. Fisk held the team record until Frank Thomas passed him in 1996. Baines rejoined the White Sox for 1996 and part of 1997, hitting 34 homers to leap back ahead of Fisk on the White Sox list. Fisk remained the top slugging catcher until May 5, 2004, when the Mets' Mike Piazza passed him by homering against San Francisco's Jerome Williams at Shea Stadium.

Roger Clemens won his 300th game and struck out his 4,000th batter *in the same game.* On June 13, 2003, Clemens pitched the Yankees to a 5-2 win over the St. Louis Cardinals at Yankee Stadium, allowing six hits and two walks in 6.2 innings while striking out ten. He entered the game with 3,996 strikeouts and started fast by striking out the side in the first and then got his 4,000th in the second when he fanned Edgar Renteria. Clemens' milestones made him the 21st pitcher to get 300 wins and just the third to reach 4,000 strikeouts.

Don Sutton was involved in all four American League match-ups of 300-win pitchers – *against three different opponents and each time at Anaheim Stadium.* In the first match-up of 300-game winners since Pud Galvin and Tim Keefe met in the National League on July 21, 1892, Sutton (301 wins) and Phil Niekro (304 wins) squared off on June 28, 1986, but neither pitcher figured in the decision. Less than a month later on July 27, 1986, Sutton won his 304th game by pitching eight shutout innings against Boston and Tom Seaver (308 wins) as the Angels won 3-0. Sutton was the loser on June 8, 1987, when paired up against Cleveland's Niekro for a second time. Seeking his 313th win, Sutton gave up just two runs in eight innings, yet Niekro earned his 315th win by hurling 7.1 innings of three-hit, shutout ball as the Tribe beat the Angels 2-0. Later that season on August 4, Sutton collected his 318th career win against 328-game winner Steve Carlton and the Twins. Sutton gave up three runs in six innings and received plenty of support as his teammates hammered Carlton for 11 hits and nine runs in 4.2 innings as the Angels won 12-3. The only NL match-up of 300-game winners since 1900 was on April 29, 2005, when the Greg Maddux and the Chicago Cubs beat Roger

Clemens and the Houston Astros by a score of 3-2. Maddux won his 306th game with a two-run, six-inning performance, nipping 329-game winner Clemens who allowed three runs in seven innings. Clemens collected two singles against Maddux, making him the only post-1900 pitcher with 300 wins to get a hit against another 300-win pitcher.

Roger Maris broke Babe Ruth's single-season home run record by hitting his 61st home run on October 1, 1961. Maris's blast came against Tracy Stallard at Yankee Stadium in the fourth inning and accounted for the only run in New York's 1-0 victory over Boston. During his historic season, Maris did not steal a base, and because Mickey Mantle batted behind him in the lineup, he did not receive a single intentional walk.

Although there have only been eight 100-stolen base seasons in baseball since 1900, Vince Coleman did it in *three consecutive years.* The Cardinals' speedy outfielder stole 110 bases as a rookie in 1985 and followed up with 107 thefts in 1986 and 109 more in 1987. During this same three-year stretch, Coleman hit only four home runs, one of which was an inside-the-park homer. Baseball's all-time stolen base leader Rickey Henderson is responsible for three of the other 100-steals season, topping the mark in 1980, 1982, and 1983 with the Oakland A's.

On September 11, 1985, Pete Rose not only broke Ty Cobb's record with his 4,192nd hit, he also scored both runs during the Reds' 2-0 win over the San Diego Padres. Rose got the record-breaking hit with a first-inning single to left against Eric Show but was eventually stranded on third base. Rose walked and scored on a ground out by Nick Esasky in the third inning and tripled and came in on Esasky's sacrifice fly in the seventh.

From 1991, his first full season in the major leagues, through 1998, Chicago White Sox slugger Frank Thomas recorded more than 100 RBIs, runs scored, and walks each season. Thomas' streak ended in 1999 when a season-ending injury in early September froze his totals at 77 RBIs, 74 runs, and 87 walks. Thomas recovered from his injury and added a ninth season in 2000 when he scored 115 runs, knocked in 143 and walked 112 times. Lou Gehrig, Babe Ruth, Barry Bonds, and Ted Williams are the only other players to have at least eight such seasons, but Thomas is the *only* player to accomplish the feat eight straight years.

Moment of Glory

Keith McDonald managed just three major league hits – *but all three were home runs*. In his first major league at-bat on July 4, 2000, for the St. Louis Cardinals, McDonald pinch-hit for Edgar Renteria and delivered an eighth-inning homer against Cincinnati's Andy Larkin. Two days later he led off the second inning with a blast against the Reds' Osvaldo Fernandez, joining Bob Nieman (September 14, 1951) as the only player to homer in his first two major league at-bats. On July 15 in his sixth career at-bat, McDonald collected his third homer, a pinch-hit shot against Jesus Pena of the White Sox in the ninth inning. McDonald went hitless in his only at-bat on July 16 and then did not bat again in the majors until September 2001 when he went 0 for 2 to end his career with three hits in nine at-bats.

Joe Astroth is among a handful of players who have driven in at least six runs in a single inning. Astroth appeared in just 39 games in 1950 and had his big inning on September 23 at Washington. The Philadelphia A's beat the Senators 16-5 by scoring 12 runs in the sixth, highlighted by Astroth's grand slam and two-run single. Astroth's grand slam came against Washington's Julio Moreno and was the first of his 13 career homers – as well as his only grand slam – and was the only home run he hit in 1950. Astroth's six-RBI inning accounted for one-third of his season's 18 RBIs.

Pittsburgh native John Wehner hit the last home run at Pittsburgh's Three Rivers Stadium on October 1, 2000, connecting for a two-run shot against Cubs' hurler Jon Lieber in the fifth inning. It was Wehner's only homer of the season in 50 at-bats and was the last of his four career homers.

Philadelphia's Jeff Grotewold hit three home runs in 65 at-bats in 1992 – and they came on *three consecutive days*, each as a pinch hitter in the seventh inning against the San Francisco Giants at Candlestick Park. He homered on July 6 against Bud Black, July 7 (in the second game of a doubleheader) against Mike Jackson, and July 8 against John Burkett. Grotewold hit only one other home run in his career.

Howie Bedell had only *one RBI* in 1968, but on June 8 he drove in the run that ended Don Drysdale's then record consecutive scoreless inning streak. Two innings after Drysdale retired Roberto Pena on a ground ball to break Walter Johnson's record of 56 straight scoreless innings, Bedell pinch-hit and delivered a fifth-inning sacrifice fly that scored Tony Taylor and ended Drysdale's streak at 58.2 innings. The RBI was just Bedell's third – *and last* – career RBI and was his first since hitting a two-run triple for Milwaukee against Pittsburgh's Tom Sturdivant at Forbes Field on May 17, 1962.

In Detroit's 12-inning, 9-8 win over Cleveland on June 21, 1970, Tigers' shortstop Cesar Gutierrez became the first modern player to get seven consecutive hits in one game. After sitting out the opener, Gutierrez started the second game of a doubleheader by looping a single to center in the first. He then singled to left in the third, singled to deep short in the fifth, doubled to left in the seventh, and forced extra innings with a two-out single to right in the eighth that tied the game 8-8. Gutierrez used the three extra frames to beat out an infield hit behind second base in the 10th and get his seventh hit with a single off the pitcher's glove in the twelfth. The next season, Gutierrez's last year in the majors, he collected a *total* of seven hits in 38 games.

Joel Youngblood is the only player to get hits for two teams in two cities in the same day – *and each hit was against a Hall of Fame pitcher.* On August 4, 1982, Youngblood was with the New York Mets and hit a two-run single in two at-bats against Chicago's Fergie Jenkins in the first three innings of an afternoon game at Wrigley Field. When told that he had just been traded to Montreal, Youngblood left the game at Wrigley and caught a quick flight to Philadelphia to join the Expos for their night game against the Phillies. He arrived in the fourth inning, was inserted into right field in the sixth, and collected an infield single in the seventh against Steve Carlton.

Mike Benjamin got just 41 hits in 186 at-bats for the San Francisco Giants in 1995 – *but collected a major league record 14 hits in a three-game span.* Benjamin began his torrid streak by collecting four singles in six at-bats against the Montreal Expos on June 11, 1995, at Candlestick Park. Two days later against the Cubs at Wrigley Field, he went 4 for 5, including a home run against Jaime Navarro. The next day, June 14, Benjamin knocked out five singles and a double in seven at-bats as the Giants beat the Cubs 4-3 in 13 innings. The 14 base hits during Benjamin's hot streak accounted for 34.1 percent his season total.

Craig Anderson was the winning pitcher in both games of the first New York Met doubleheader sweep – *and then never won another game in the majors.* After splitting the first twin bill in franchise history on April 29, 1962, against the Phillies, the Mets played their second doubleheader against the Milwaukee Braves at the Polo Grounds on May 12. In the first game Anderson pitched the eighth and ninth innings in relief, allowing just one hit. Braves' starter Warren Spahn, looking for his 313th career victory, entered the bottom of the ninth with a 2-1 lead. Spahn allowed a leadoff single to Gil Hodges but retired the next two Mets before Hobie Landrith homered into the right field bleachers to end the game and make Anderson the winning pitcher. In the second game with the score tied at 7-7, Anderson was summoned from the bullpen to pitch the ninth inning, and he retired the Braves in order. Gil Hodges then hit a one-out, solo homer against Hank Fischer in the bottom of the ninth, giving Anderson another win. The two victories raised Anderson's record to 3-1, but that proved to be the highlight of his career as he would lose his next 16 decisions to finish the year 3-17.

Anderson returned with the Mets in 1963 and was 0-2 in three games and was 0-1 in four games in 1964, ending his career with a record of 7-23.

In his only career start, Don Fisher got his only career victory – *by pitching a 13-inning complete-game shutout.* After pitching five innings of relief in his first game on August 25, 1945, Fisher pitched in his second, and final, major league game for the New York Giants on September 30 against Boston at Braves Field. In the first game of a doubleheader, Fisher gave up ten hits and three walks while going the distance in the Giants' 1-0 win. The Giants banged out just six hits, but one was Nap Reyes' solo homer off Don Hendrickson in the top of the 13th to account for the game's only run. Due to the length of the first game, the second game was called due to darkness at the end of seven innings with the score tied 2-2.

On July 19, 1955, Detroit's rookie pitcher Babe Birrer hit the only two homers and drove in the only six runs of his career – *in a game in which he was not the winning pitcher.* With the Tigers clinging to a 5-4 lead in the sixth and Baltimore with runner on second with nobody out, Birrer was summoned from the bullpen to squash the Orioles' rally. He kept the tying run off the scoreboard and in the bottom of the inning made the score 8-4 with a three-run homer against George Zuverink. Two innings later he smacked another three-run blast (this time against Art Schallock) to make the final score 12-4. Despite Birrer's big day at the plate and four scoreless innings on the mound, starter Frank Lary was credited with the win. In his three-year career Birrer appeared in 56 games, compiling a 4-3 record and collecting seven hits in 27 at-bats.

Robin Jennings' career was just 93 games from 1996 to 2001, producing only two triples, three homers and 24 RBIs. Jennings did have one big game on August 31, 2001, leading the Reds to an 11-3 win over the Pirates. After flying out to left in the second inning, he hit a bases-loaded triple to center in the fourth against Pittsburgh's Todd Ritchie and followed with a grand slam against Damaso Marte in the next inning.

On October 2, 2005, Chris Duncan hit the last regular season home run at Busch Stadium in St. Louis – *which was also his first career home run*. In just his 10th career at-bat, Duncan, the son of Cardinals' pitching coach Dave Duncan, pinch-hit for pitcher Brad Thompson and went deep against Cincinnati's Brandon Claussen in the fifth to break a 5-5 tie. The Cardinals added another run later as they won their 100th game of the year.

On June 30, 1979, Mike Vail hit his only career grand slam, a pinch-hit homer in the bottom of the 11th inning – *in a game that his team lost*. Tied at 3-3 with the Cubs at the end of nine, the Mets exploded for six runs in the top of the 11th on two-run homers by Joel Youngblood and Lee Mazzilli and a two-run triple by Steve Henderson. In the bottom of the inning, the Cubs came roaring back with a run to make the score 9-4 and had the bases loaded when Vail was called upon to hit for pitcher Donnie Moore. He delivered a grand slam off Dale Murray to pull the Cubs to within one run, but Ed Glynn relieved Murray and retired the next two Cubs to preserve the win.

On October 4, 1992, the last day of the season, San Francisco's Greg Litton hit a pinch-hit grand slam in the 13th inning off Cincinnati's Scott Ruskin to beat the Reds 6-2. It was the only grand slam and only extra-inning homer of Litton's 13 career home runs.

The only player since 1900 to go 7 for 7 at the plate in a nine-inning game is Rennie Stennett. Batting leadoff on September 16, 1975, the Pirates' second baseman collected four singles, two doubles, and a triple in the Pirates 22-0 thrashing of the Cubs at Wrigley Field. Stennett collected two hits in both the first and fifth innings, making him just the fourth player to get two hits in an inning twice in one game. In the next game Stennett collected three more singles against the Phillies to give him a record ten base hits over a two-game span – a feat matched by Kirby Puckett on August 29 and 30 in 1987.

On June 8, 1989, Philadelphia fell behind Pittsburgh 10-0 in the first inning but rallied to win 15-11. The Phillies' comeback was helped by back-up second baseman Steve Jeltz who entered the game in the second inning, replacing starter Tommy Herr. Jeltz walked and scored in the third, hit a two-run homer batting lefthanded against Bob Walk in the fifth, and smacked a three-run shot batting righthanded against Bob Kipper in the sixth. Jeltz would finish his career with only five home runs in 1,749 at-bats.

Jack Reed's *only* career home run in 129 at-bats provided the margin of victory in New York's 22-inning victory at Tiger Stadium on June 24, 1962. Tigers' starter Frank Lary entered the game with a 28-11 record against New York, but the Yankees exploded for six runs in the first, highlighted by Clete Boyer's three-run homer, and added one more before Lary was removed following the second inning. Rookie Purnal Goldy put the Tigers on the board with a three-run blast (the last of his three career homers) in the bottom of the first, and they added three more in the third before finally tying the game 7-7 in the sixth on a single by Rocky Colavito. Marshall Bridges, Tex Clevenger, Bud Daley and Jim Bouton combined to hold Detroit scoreless the rest of the way despite a close call in the 11th when Colavito opened with a triple. Following two intentional walks to load the bases, the Yankees got Chico Fernandez on short line drive to left and ended the Tiger's threat by turning an easy double play on a botched suicide squeeze bunt by Dick Brown. Reed, who had entered the game for defensive purposes in the 13th, finally broke New York's 19-inning scoreless streak with a one-out, two-run homer into the lower left field stands against Phil Regan to put New York ahead 9-7. Jim Bouton, who pitched the last seven innings, retired the Tigers in the bottom of the inning (despite giving up Colavito's seventh hit of the game) to earn his second career victory.

Although he hit just 12 homers in 330 at-bats in 2003, Jeff DaVanon tied a major league record by hitting two homers in three consecutive games for the Angels. DaVanon began his power surge on June 1 at Tampa Bay when he connected in the third and fifth innings against Carlos Reyes. The Angels' next series was against in Montreal Expos with the games being played in San Juan, Puerto Rico at Estadio Hiram Bithorn. DaVanon started the series by homering against Tomo Ohka in the first inning and Scott Stewart in the ninth and stayed hot in the next game, getting round-trippers in the sixth inning off Dan Smith and in the eighth against Joey Eischen. DaVanon's streak ended the next day as he went 0 for 5.

Rick Dempsey hit just four homers in 151 at-bats in 1989 – *but one of them ended the second longest 1-0 game in major league history.* With the Dodgers and Expos scoreless at the end of 21 innings on August 23, 1989, Dempsey led off the top of the 22nd and hit a 2-1 pitch from Montreal's Dennis Martinez over the left field fence to finally put a run on the board. In the bottom of the frame, Dempsey ended the game by throwing out Rex Hudler trying to steal second. The game ended two innings short of the 1-0, 24-inning marathon between New York and Houston on April 15, 1968.

Bill Salkeld had only two career triples in 850 at-bats – *but managed to hit for the cycle.* On August 4, 1945, Salkeld personally staked the Pirates to a 5-1 lead at Forbes Field with a three-run homer in the first of Blix Donnelly and a two-run triple in the seventh. Salkeld also had a double and two singles, but the Cardinals rallied to tie the score in the eighth and pushed across a run in the ninth to win 6-5.

Bob Brenly had a game to remember when the San Francisco Giants took on the Atlanta Braves on September 14, 1986, at Candlestick Park. Brenly, primarily the Giants' starting catcher, was playing third base, and he committed four errors in the fourth inning, which led to four unearned runs. Brenly began his redemption by hitting a solo homer against Charlie Puleo in the fifth. He followed that with a run-scoring single in the seventh and then capped the Giants' comeback by hitting a solo homer off Paul Assenmacher with two outs in the bottom of the ninth to win the game 7-6. Brenly's big game was his *only* multi-homer game of 1986.

Mike Hegan batted 218 times in 80 games for the Milwaukee Brewers in 1976, and collected just four doubles, three triples, and five home runs – but got *one of each* to hit for the cycle against the Detroit Tigers at Tiger Stadium on September 3. The triple was the last of his career, and Hegan would get only one more double and two more homers before retiring following the 1977 season.

On May 23, 2002, at Milwaukee's Miller Park, Shawn Green had the game of his life – hitting four homers, a double and a single and driving in seven runs as the Dodgers cruised to an easy 16-3 victory. Green began his offensive assault with an RBI double to right field in the first inning and then hit a two-run shot in the second-inning homer against Glendon Rusch, before hammering solo homers in the fourth and fifth innings off reliever Brian Mallette. Green picked up a single to center field in the eighth but seemed unlikely to bat in the top of the ninth inning until Adrian Beltre homered in front of him with two outs to give the Dodgers' outfielder one more chance. Green took advantage of his opportunity by hitting his fourth homer, this one coming off Jose Cabrera. He ended the game 6 for 6 – becoming the first player with six hits and four homers in the same game – and had 19 total bases, breaking Joe Adcock's 1954 record.

Colorado's Mike Lansing hit for the cycle *during the first four innings* of the Rockies' 19-2 rout of the Diamondbacks on June 18, 2000, at Coors Field. The Rockies jumped on Arizona starter Armando Reynoso by getting two runs in the first, including an RBI triple from Lansing. In the second inning, Lansing capped a three-run rally with a two-run homer against Reynoso. Colorado exploded for nine runs in the third with Lansing contributing a double and two RBIs against Omar Daal. He completed the cycle in the fourth with a single against Russ Springer.

On August 8, 1998, Ray Lankford struck out five consecutive times against the Chicago Cubs – *but ended up the game's hero.* After failing to make contact in the first nine innings, Lankford hit a two-run homer with two outs in the 11th against Cubs' ace reliever Rod Beck to tie the game. He later got the game-winning single against Dave Stevens in the 13th as the Cardinals rallied to beat the Cubs 9-8.

Pitcher Livan Hernandez, a career .237 hitter as of the 2005 season, was 11 for 12 at the plate over a four-game stretch in 2001

– with two doubles, a home run, three RBIs and six runs scored. Hernandez started his hot streak on July 26 by going 3 for 3 with a double against Curt Schilling. He then went 2 for 3 against the Pirates on July 31 and followed that with a 3-for-3 day, including a double and two runs, against the Phillies on August 5. Hernandez capped his hot streak by going 4 for 4 with a homer and three RBIs and scoring three runs against the Cubs at Wrigley Field on August 11.

No-Hitters

Hideo Nomo's two career no-hitters are the *only* no-hit games pitched at two different ballparks. The Colorado Rockies moved into hitter-friendly Coors Field for the 1995 season, and the park's lone no-hit game was played on September 17, 1996, when Nomo struck out eight Rockies and won 9-0. Baltimore's Camden Yards opened for the 1992 season and has hosted just one no-hitter, which was on April 4, 2001, when Nomo whiffed 11 batters and beat the Orioles 3-0.

Rookie Nick Maddox, making just his third career start, threw the first no-hitter in Pirates' history, a 2-1 victory against Brooklyn at Exposition Park in Pittsburgh on September 20, 1907. Less than two years later, the Pirates moved to Forbes Field on June 30, 1909, and stayed through June 28, 1970, playing a total of 4,760 games without being involved in a no-hitter (win or lose) during their stay there. Just over a year after leaving Forbes Field, the Pirates were no-hit in their new home, Three Rivers Stadium, on August 14, 1971, by Bob Gibson of St. Louis.

Tim Hulett played for the losing team in two no-hit games *during his first eight games in the majors.* The 23-year-old rookie appeared in six games with the Chicago White Sox at the end of the 1983 season, the fourth of which was a no-hitter by Oakland's Mike Warren on September 29. Hulett was 0 for 2 before being lifted for a pinch hitter in the ninth inning. On April 7, 1984, Hulett's second game of the young season was as a defensive replacement for starting third baseman Van Law in the eighth inning of a no-hitter by Detroit's Jack Morris at Comiskey Park. Hulett also took part in Joe Cowley's no-hitter against the Angels on September 19, 1986, going 1 for 4 and scoring a run.

Jeff Torborg was the catcher behind the plate for Sandy Koufax's 1-0 perfect game against the Cubs on September 9, 1965, and also caught Nolan Ryan's first no-hitter, a 3-0 victory against Kansas City on May 15, 1973.

Detroit's Virgil Trucks won only five games during the 1952 season – *but pitched two no-hitters.* Trucks no-hit the Washington Senators at Tiger Stadium on May 15 and held New York hitless at Yankee Stadium on August 25, winning each game 1-0. Trucks finished the season with a record of 5-19 and a 3.97 ERA.

The last three pitchers to no-hit the San Francisco Giants were named "Kevin" – *and they are the only three pitchers named "Kevin" to ever throw a no-hitter.* The trio of hurlers who held the Giants hitless are Kevin Gross (August 17, 1992, at Dodger Stadium), Kevin Brown (June 10, 1997, at Candlestick Park), and Kevin Millwood (April 27, 2003 at Veterans Stadium).

Yankee Stadium served as the site for all three interleague no-hitters. New York pitcher Don Larsen threw his famous perfect World Series game there against the Brooklyn Dodgers on October 8, 1956, and Yankees' southpaw David Wells also hurled a perfect game at the Stadium on May 17, 1998, against the Expos. Larsen and Wells not only each threw a perfect game for New York – *they graduated from the same high school.* Larsen is a 1947 graduate of Point Loma High School in San Diego, and Wells was a member of the class of 1982. The Yankees were on the losing side of the third interleague no-hitter when the NL's Houston Astros used a record six pitchers to no-hit the them on their home field on June 11, 2003.

Only once since 1900 have two no-hitters occurred on the same day. Oakland's Dave Stewart held the Blue Jays hitless in a 5-0 win at Toronto on June 29, 1990, and later that night Dodgers' lefthander

Fernando Valenzuela pitched a 6-0 no-hitter against St. Louis at Dodger Stadium.

Despite being the only pitcher to throw consecutive no-hitters, Johnny Vander Meer finished his career with *a losing record*. The 23-year-old Cincinnati southpaw threw his first no-hitter against Boston at Crosley Field on June 11, 1938, winning by a score of 3-0. In his next start on June 15, Vander Meer became the first of four pitchers (and still the only National League pitcher) to throw two no-hit games in a season by beating the Brooklyn Dodgers with a 6-0 masterpiece in the first night game played at Ebbets Field. Vander Meer showed that he was also handy with the bat by getting one hit in each game. Vander Meer finished his 13-year career in 1951 with a record of 119-121.

Pittsburgh's Francisco Cordova and Ricardo Rincon held the Houston Astros hitless for ten innings at Three Rivers Stadium on July 12, 1997 – the only time that two pitchers have combined to throw an extra-inning no-hitter. Cordova pitched the first nine innings and left with the game still scoreless. Rincon pitched a hitless 10th inning and was the winner when Mark Smith belted a three-run homer against Houston's John Hudek in the bottom of the frame.

Bobo Holloman's entire major league career consisted of a 3-7 record in 22 games for the 1953 St. Louis Browns, but on May 6 – *in his first starting assignment* – he no-hit the Philadelphia A's 6-0. No pitcher with fewer career wins has thrown a no-hitter.

Addie Joss is the only pitcher to throw two no-hitters against the same team. Joss pitched a perfect game against the Chicago White Sox in Cleveland on October 2, 1908, and threw the major league's next no-hitter when held them hitless again in Chicago on April 20, 1910. He won both games by the score of 1-0.

The Houston Astros set the record for most pitchers used in a no-hitter (using six, breaking the previous record of four) when they beat the New York Yankees on June 11, 2003. Houston starter Roy

Oswalt left with an injury after just one inning and was followed by Pete Munro (2.2 innings), Kirk Saarloos (1.1 innings), Brad Lidge (2 innings), Octavio Dotel (1 inning), and Billy Wagner (1 inning). The Yankees had entered the game with a record streak of 6,890 straight games without being no-hit since last being held hitless by Baltimore's Hoyt Wilhelm on September 20, 1958. Although it is not listed in the record book as an official no-hitter, Melido Perez did hold New York hitless in a rain-shortened, six-inning game on September 20, 1990.

The New York Mets joined the National League in 1962 and have yet to have a pitcher throw a no-hitter. Mets' pitchers have posted several one-hitters and some of their pitchers – Nolan Ryan (who had seven), Tom Seaver, Mike Scott, Dwight Gooden, David Cone and Hideo Nomo – threw no-hitters *after* leaving the Mets. In sharp contrast, a Montreal Expo pitcher hurled a no-hitter in just the *ninth* game in the franchise's history. After just two wins in 46 games (but only two starts) with the Cubs in 1967 and 1968, Bill Stoneman was selected by the Expos in the December 1968 expansion draft. Following Montreal's win in their first game at New York, Stoneman took the hill on April 9, 1969, and was handed the Expos' first loss when he was pounded for four earned runs in only one-third of an inning. Four days later he suffered another loss when the Cubs got seven runs, only one of which was earned, against him in 8.2 innings at Wrigley Field. Stoneman's next start was on April 17, on the road against the Phillies. He fanned eight and walked five while holding Philadelphia hitless and won 7-0 for his first victory since September 26, 1967. Stoneman added another no-hitter, again by a 7-0 score, to his record on October 2, 1972, against the Mets in the opening game of a doubleheader but still finished his career with a losing record of 53-77.

On August 26, 1916, Philadelphia A's pitcher Joe Bush threw a no-hitter against Cleveland – *just one day after they knocked him out of a game in the third inning.* In the August 25 contest, Bush gave up six hits plus two walks and was removed for a pinch hitter in the bottom of the third, trailing 5-0. The 1916 A's were a dreadful team, finishing the season 36-117, so Bush was able to persuade manager Connie Mack to give him another chance. He started the next game by walking leadoff hitter Jack Graney but then retired the next 27 straight and won 5-0.

Joe Cowley is the only pitcher whose last career win was a no-hitter. Cowley was with the White Sox when he held the Angels hitless on September 19, 1986. The 7-1 win raised his record to 11-9, but he went 0-2 in his next three starts to finish the year at 11-11. Shortly before the beginning of the 1987 season, Cowley was traded to the Phillies where he was 0-4 with a 15.43 ERA in just 11.2 innings. He ended his career with 33-25 record.

Oddities

Within the span of five at-bats, Moises Alou hit three, three-run homers against Orel Hershiser – *in three different ballparks.* Alou began his assault on Hershiser at Florida's Pro Player Stadium in Game 1 of the 1997 World Series with a homer in the fourth inning that hit the left field foul pole and gave the Marlins a 4-1 lead on their way to a 7-4 win. In Game 5 at Cleveland's Jacobs Field, Alou smacked a sixth-inning, three-run shot in his third at-bat against Hershiser, giving Florida a 5-4 lead and propelling them to a 8-7 victory. During the off-season both players would change teams, with Alou going to the Houston Astros and Hershiser joining the San Francisco Giants. In their first confrontation of the 1998 season, Alou blasted a three-run homer against Hershiser in the first inning at the Astrodome on April 1.

Calvin Pickering homered in three consecutive at-bats – *over a span of almost three years.* Pickering connected for a pinch-hit homer for Boston on October 5, 2001, at Baltimore against John Wasdin. After spending 2002 and 2003 in the minors, Pickering finally made it back to the big leagues with Kansas City on August 22, 2004. After walking in his first plate appearance, he drove a 3-2 offering from Texas pitcher Scott Erickson over the fence in left in the third inning. Two innings later Pickering smashed the first pitch from Joaquin Benoit to dead center field for a two-run homer. His home run streak ended in his next at-bat when he lined out to second.

Warren Spahn finished his pitching career with 363 wins – *and also got 363 hits as a batter.* Spahn had 356 wins and 356 hits in his 20 years with the Braves. In his last season of 1965, he began the year with the Mets and won four games and rapped out four more hits before being released by New York and signing with the San Francisco Giants, where he won three more games and knocked out another three hits. Spahn also had appeared in eight World Series games – collecting four wins and four hits.

Jimmie Foxx won three batting titles (1932, 1933 and 1938) and also won the American League MVP award each of those years. By contrast, Ted Williams won seven batting titles, including titles in 1942 and 1947 when he won the Triple Crown, but his MVP awards came in 1946 and 1949 – years in which he did not win the batting title. Williams finished second in the MVP voting four times in the seven years in which he won batting titles.

Despite seven 30-HR seasons and six 100-RBI seasons, Reggie Jackson never hit 30 homers or drove 100 runs in consecutive seasons. Jackson surpassed 30 home runs and 100 RBIs in 1969, 1973, and 1975 with Oakland, in 1977 and 1980 with New York, and in 1982 with California. He also hit 32 homers (but only 80 RBIs) with Oakland in 1971.

Warren Spahn, who wore #21 for the Braves, had eight different seasons in which he won exactly 21 games. Spahn won 21 games in 1947, 1949, 1950, 1954, 1957, 1959, 1960 and 1961. In 1958 he won his last start of the year to finish with 22 wins, preventing himself from winning exactly 21 games for five consecutive years.

Pitcher Dave Eiland achieved the unique feat of giving up a homer to the first batter he faced in the majors and homering in his first at-bat. In his major league debut on August 3, 1988, Eiland gave up a homer to Paul Molitor leading off the bottom of the first at County Stadium in Milwaukee. After being released following his fourth season with the Yankees, Eiland signed with the San Diego Padres and hit a two-run home run against Bobby Ojeda on April 10, 1992, at Jack Murphy Stadium in his first time at the plate. Eiland was 0-2 with a 5.67 ERA in seven games in 1992 – *finishing the season with more homers than wins.*

There have been only 12 unassisted triple plays in major league history, *but the feat was once performed on successive days.* Chicago Cub shortstop Jimmy Cooney executed an unassisted triple play in the fourth inning against the Pittsburgh Pirates on May 30, 1927. The next day, Johnny Neun was playing first base for the Detroit Tigers and ended the game with an unassisted triple play in the ninth inning against the Cleveland Indians. Cooney had been one of the baserunners when Glenn Wright pulled off an unassisted triple play during the ninth inning of Pittsburgh's game against the St. Louis Cardinals on May 7, 1925.

Speedster Herb Washington, signed by Oakland A's owner Charlie O. Finley as a pinch runner, appeared in 105 games for the A's during the 1974 and 1975 seasons, stealing 31 bases and scoring 33 runs – *but never batted once.*

In the 1957 season, Milwaukee Brave Wes Covington batted 328 times, walloping 21 home runs and eight triples – *but only four doubles.* The only other player with a season of at least 20 homers and four doubles is Mark McGwire who hit 29 homers and four doubles in 2001. Although he hit more homers than Covington, McGwire got 37 fewer hits (56 to 93) and did not hit a triple.

Enzo Hernandez batted 549 times for the 1971 San Diego Padres and drove in only 12 runs. He collected 122 hits including nine doubles and three triples but did not homer. No player has batted 425 or more times in a season and driven in fewer runs.

Johnnie LeMaster played for three last-place teams in 1985 – *each of which lost more than 100 games.* LeMaster started the year with the San Francisco Giants who would finish the year 62-100. After playing in 12 games and batting 16 times without a hit, he was traded on May 7 to a Cleveland Indian squad that would finish the season at 60-102. With the Tribe, LeMaster batted 20 times in 11 games, collecting three singles before being traded to the Pittsburgh Pirates on May 30. As a Pirate, he played in 22 games and got nine hits in 58 at-bats, including his last home run, for a Pittsburgh team that ended the year with a 57-104 record.

Robin Yount drove in exactly 77 runs in three successive seasons (1990-1992).

From 1993 to 1996, Milwaukee's Cal Eldred was *literally* a .500 pitcher, compiling records of 16-16, 11-11, 1-1, and 4-4. By winning his last start of the 1997 season on September 25, Eldred would have evened his 1997 record at 14-14 and kept his steak alive, but he lost 2-1 to Kansas City (despite giving up only two runs in eight innings) and ended the season at 13-15.

On April 9, 1994, Paul Molitor got his 2,500th hit and Joe Carter knocked in his 1,000th run – *and they did it hitting the same ball.* With Seattle and Toronto tied at 6-6 in the bottom of the ninth, Molitor singled against Seattle's Bobby Thigpen for his 2,500th hit. Unaware of his accomplishment, he did not ask to keep the ball as a souvenir and two pitches later his teammate Joe Carter hit the same ball for a two-run, game-winning homer and collected his 1,000th and 1,001st RBIs in the process. The fan who caught the ball later returned it to Carter.

As part of his then record streak of 172 consecutive errorless games by a catcher, Charles Johnson played the entire 1997 season without an error – but then made an error in *the first inning of the first game of the 1998 season.* His streak ended when he threw wildly to second base as he attempted to throw out the Cubs' Mickey Morandini.

Colorado third baseman Vinny Castilla was the model of consistency in 1996 and 1997 when he put together two remarkably similar years:

	G	H	HR	TB	R	RBI	Avg.	Slg.
1996	160	191	40	345	97	113	.304	.548
1997	159	186	40	335	94	113	.304	.547

During his 200th career win on August 18, 1998, Greg Maddux's teammates supported him by getting nine hits – *all of which were doubles*. Walt Weiss, Gerald Williams, and Danny Bautista each doubled twice and Andres Galarraga, Chipper Jones and Eddie Perez added one each as Maddux allowed just one earned run in seven innings, beating the Giants 8-4 at Turner Field.

Ricky Gutierrez had a batting average of .261 for Houston for three consecutive seasons. He was 79 for 303 in 1997, 128 for 491 in 1998, and 70 for 268 in 1999.

Although they combined to hit just five inside-the-park homer runs in their careers, Toby Harrah and Bump Wills hit inside-the-park home runs on *consecutive pitches* at Yankee Stadium on August 27, 1977. In the seventh inning with two men on, Harrah drove a pitch from Ken Clay to right field that went off Lou Piniella's glove and rolled away, allowing Harrah to circle the bases. The speedy Wills then stepped into the batter's box and hit Clay's next pitch over the head of center fielder Mickey Rivers for another inside-the-parker.

Chick Fullis had 200 hits for the 1933 Philadelphia Phillies – *but never collected over 100 hits in any other season*. His next highest total was 99 hits for the 1931 New York Giants, and he ended his career in 1936 with just 548 base hits.

Warren Spahn pitched for two teams managed by Casey Stengel – *but they came 23 years apart*. Spahn made his major league debut on April 19, 1942, with Stengel's Boston Braves but spent most of the season in the minor leagues before being recalled late in the year, and he did not record a decision in four games. Spahn was away serving in World War II while Stengel managed part of the 1943 season and did not return to the team until the 1946 season, long after Stengel was out as the Braves' skipper. Their paths crossed again in 1965 when the Hall of Fame lefthander was sold by the Braves, now in Milwaukee, to Stengel's New York Mets. Spahn compiled a record of 4-12 for Stengel before being released in July and catching on with the San Francisco Giants where he was 3-4 to finish his career.

On May 11, 1999, two pitchers with the same name opposed each other for the only time in the twentieth century. Colorado's Bobby M. Jones beat Bobby J. Jones of the New York Mets at Coors Field by the score of 8-5. Bobby J. pitched 5.1 innings and was charged with eight earned runs while Bobby M. pitched into the sixth, allowing two runs, just one of which was earned.

Only three players have swiped a base in four different decades. Two are speedsters Rickey Henderson (1,406 career steals) and Tim Raines (808 career steals). The third player is Ted Williams – who stole just 23 bases in his 19-year career. Williams swiped two bags as a rookie in 1939, 14 in the 1940s, seven in the 1950s and one in 1960.

On July 29, 1996, Houston's Mike Hampton defeated Cincinnati's Mark Portugal to improve his record to 7-7, with the loss dropping Portugal's record to 7-7. Hampton pitched seven innings while Portugal pitched 7.1 innings and gave up seven hits. Houston's Billy Wagner got the save, his seventh of the season.

Vic Power had just three stolen bases in 1958 (and only 45 steals in 1,627 career games) – *but he stole home twice in one game.* Power entered Cleveland's game against Detroit on August 14 with just eight career steals before stealing home against pitcher Bill Fischer in the eighth inning to cap a five-run rally and give the Indians a 9-7 lead. The Tigers rallied to retie the game only to have Power steal home again, this time with two outs in the bottom of the 10th against Tiger hurler Frank Lary to win the game 10-9. His two thefts of home plate against Detroit were Power's only steals for the Indians in 93 games in 1958, his other steal coming earlier in the season when he was with the Kansas City A's. Power is the last player to steal home twice in one game.

Mel Roach played sparingly in eight seasons from 1953 to 1962, collecting 119 hits in 499 at-bats for a .239 average. Somehow, Roach managed to never hit in the .200s – his season batting average was over .300 twice and under .200 the other six times.

Mike Morgan compiled a record of five wins, five losses, and five saves for the 2000 Arizona Diamondbacks. He also allowed 55 runs, all of which were earned.

The Pittsburgh Pirates' single-season stolen base record was broken in four consecutive seasons. Max Carey pilfered 63 bases for the Bucs in 1916 and held the record until Frank Taveras swiped 70 bases in 1977. Omar Moreno then set the team record each of the next three years, stealing 71 bases in 1978, topping that with 77 steals in 1979, and then swiping 96 more in 1980. Moreno's 96 steals were second to Ron LeFlore's 97 thefts, making Moreno the only player to steal over 90 bases and not lead his league.

Gaylord Perry was the last man to win 20 games for *both* the Cleveland Indians and the San Diego Padres. He was 21-13 for Cleveland in 1974 and 21-6 for San Diego in 1978.

Mike Boddicker was traded for both a future 50-homer hitter and a future 300-strikeout pitcher – *in the same trade.* Boddicker was dealt from the Baltimore Orioles to the Boston Red Sox for Brady Anderson and Curt Schilling on July 29, 1988. Anderson would later hit 50 homers for the O's in 1996, and Schilling would post strikeout totals of 319 in 1997 and 300 in 1998 for Philadelphia.

Only two players have scored more than 150 runs while hitting fewer than 32 homers – *and they did it on the same team.* Woody English (14 homers, 152 runs) and Kiki Cuyler (13 homers, 155 runs) both did it in 1930 for the Chicago Cubs. Cuyler hit .355 and English hit .335 as the pair got on base often enough to allow Hack Wilson to drive in a major league record 191 runs that season.

Luis Castillo hit .334 (180 for 539) for the Florida Marlins in 2000 but managed to drive in only 17 runs. Castillo hit only one home run and batted just .211 (19 for 90) with runners in scoring position. No other player with at least 500 at-bats has hit at least .300 and driven in fewer runs in a season.

Los Angeles Dodgers' first baseman Eddie Murray led all major league players in 1990 with a .330 batting average – *but did not win a batting crown.* George Brett finished just below Murray and took the American League batting title with a .329 average. In the National League, Willie McGee qualified for the NL batting crown by hitting .335 in 501 at-bats with St. Louis before being traded to Oakland in late August. McGee hit just .274 in 113 at-bats with the A's against American League pitching, lowering his overall season average to .324.

Despite just 13 lifetime triples, John Olerud hit for the cycle *twice.* In the Mets' 9-5 victory over the Expos on September 11, 1997, Olerud had an RBI double in the first inning, a single in the third, and a homer off the right field foul pole in the seventh. He stepped in the batter's box in the bottom of the eighth with the bases loaded and smashed rookie Steve Kline's second pitch at center fielder Vladimir Guerrero. Guerrero, normally a right fielder and playing with a bad hamstring, had trouble going back on the ball which went over his head and off the wall. The ball struck him and bounced away, allowing all three runners to score and Olerud to cruise into third with his first triple since August 11, 1994. On June 16, 2001, the Mariners routed the Padres 9-2 at San Diego with Olerud leading the way. After a double in the second, he tripled down the right field line in the third inning for his first three-bagger since July 9, 1998. Olerud picked up a single in the fifth and capped his big night with a long, ninth-inning homer into the upper deck in right field. The triple that Olerud collected in each of his cycles was the only triple he hit that season.

Since 1900 the Dodgers have five 100-win seasons (1941, 1942, 1953, 1962, and 1974) but did not win the World Series any of those years. The Dodgers' six World Series titles came in 1955, 1959, 1963, 1965, 1981, and 1988.

The record of 12 total home runs in one game has been accomplished twice – *and each time involved the same teams.* On May 28, 1995, the Chicago White Sox beat the Detroit Tigers 14-12 at

Tiger Stadium. Kirk Gibson, Chad Curtis, and Cecil Fielder each homered twice for the Tigers and Lou Whitaker added one. For Chicago, Ron Karkovice hit two, and Ray Durham, Craig Grebeck, and Frank Thomas contributed one each. Durham's homer was the first of his career, and Grebeck's four-bagger was his only one of the 1995 season. Both of Fielder's homers were three-run shots, but the other ten were all solo homers. Ironically, the previous day the White Sox had edged the Tigers in a 1-0 pitcher's duel. On July 2, 2002, the clubs met at Comiskey Park and the White Sox pounded the Tigers 17-9. Each team hit six homers – Magglio Ordonez (two), Sandy Alomar, Jr. (two), Kenny Lofton and Jose Valentin for Chicago; Dmitri Young (two), Robert Fick, George Lombard, Wendell Magee and Damion Easley for Detroit. Frank Thomas and Ray Durham played in both contests, each homering in the first game but neither hitting one in the second.

St. Louis Cardinals' lefthander Larry Jaster tied for the National League lead with five shutouts in 1966 – *with all five coming against the Los Angeles Dodgers.* After pitching one perfect inning against them in his big league debut on September 17, 1965, at Busch Stadium, Jaster dominated the Dodgers in 1966. He blanked them on April 25, July 3, and August 19 at Los Angeles and on July 29 and September 28 at St. Louis. Jaster's first start of the 1967 season was against the Dodgers on April 14 at Busch Stadium, and he held them scoreless until two men were out in the seventh when they scored on a sacrifice fly to end his scoreless streak against them at 52.2 innings.

Randy Flores earned his first career save by throwing just one pitch – *which wasn't even a strike.* On June 14, 2002, Flores entered the game in the bottom of the ninth to face Orlando Merced with a runner on first, two men out, and Texas ahead of Houston 9-6. His first pitch missed the plate, but Texas catcher Ivan Rodriguez picked Richard Hidalgo off first base to end the game.

Joe Torre set the NL record and tied the major league record by hitting into four double plays against Houston at Shea Stadium on July 21, 1975, each time erasing Felix Millan who had singled in front of him all four times. Torre hit double-play grounders to pitcher Ken Forsch in the first, shortstop Roger Metzger in the third, second baseman Larry Milbourne in the sixth, and Metzger again in the eighth.

Mike Squires appeared in 143 games, mostly at first base, for the 1983 Chicago White Sox – *but batted just 153 times.* Squires collected 34 hits, including one triple and one homer, and had 11 RBIs. Squires' 34 hits and 153 at-bats are by far the fewest of anyone who ever appeared in 140 or more games in a season. In second place are Rafael Belliard, who had 60 hits in 144 games for the 1992 Atlanta Braves, and Michael Tucker, who batted 270 times in 148 games for the 2000 Cincinnati Reds.

On April 6, 2002, Dodger pitcher Jesse Orosco walked and eventually crossed the plate when Brian Jordan blasted a grand slam. Orosco's run was his first in *almost 16 years* and was just the third, and final, run of his 24-year career. Orosco had last scored in the 14th inning of New York's 6-3 win over Cincinnati on July 22, 1986.

Despite playing 89.7 percent (1,963 of 2,189) of his games for American League teams, Joe Carter collected three milestone hits at Veterans Stadium against the NL's Philadelphia Phillies. As a rookie with the Cubs, Carter single against Steve Carlton for his first big league hit on August 1, 1983. After spending 1984 to 1989 in the AL with Cleveland, Carter was traded to San Diego and got his 1,000th hit against Phillies' pitcher Jose DeJesus on September 2, 1990. From 1991 to 1997, Carter was back in the AL with Toronto, but due to interleague play he collected his 2,000th hit off Philadelphia's Mark Leiter on June 15, 1997. Carter's first 85 games of the 1998 season were in the AL with Baltimore before a trade to San Francisco allowed him to play his final 41 games in the NL before he retired.

On April 14, 1953, Billy Bruton homered with one out in the bottom of the 10th inning against Cardinals' pitcher Gerry Staley to lift Warren Spahn and the Milwaukee Braves to a 3-2 win in their first game in their new home, County Stadium. Bruton would finish the season with 151 games played, 613 at-bats, and just that one home run.

On May 18, 1969, the Minnesota Twins victimized Tiger catcher Bill Freehan by stealing five bases in the second inning – *including two steals of home with the same batter at the plate.* Cesar Tovar singled off Detroit's Mickey Lolich, was awarded second base on a balk, and then stole third. Rod Carew followed with a walk. With Harmon Killebrew at the plate, the Twins pulled a double steal with Carew swiping second and Tovar taking home. Carew then pilfered both third and home before Killebrew struck out. Minnesota did not score again and lost 8-2.

Elmer Valo moved with three different franchises. Valo went with the A's when they moved from Philadelphia to Kansas City following the 1954 season. After playing the 1957 season with the Dodgers in Brooklyn, Valo headed west with them for the 1958 season in Los Angeles. He was also with the Washington Senators in 1960 when the moved to Minnesota and became the Twins for the 1961 campaign.

Detroit Tiger Harry Heilmann won American League batting titles in four consecutive odd-numbered years. Heilmann led the AL in 1921, 1923, 1925, and 1927 with averages of .394, .403, .393, and .398.

Bud Harrelson hit seven home runs in 4,744 career at-bats – *each one coming in a different park and in a different season.* Harrelson connected at Forbes Field (August 17, 1967), Shea Stadium (April 17, 1970), Candlestick Park (May 1, 1972), Riverfront Stadium (May 27, 1974), Fulton County Stadium (May 11, 1976), Veterans Stadium (May 29, 1977), and Arlington Stadium (June 18, 1980).

In the 2002 season, the Cleveland Indians recorded just two complete-game shutouts and the Montreal Expos had only one – *and the same pitcher threw all three games.* Bartolo Colon pitched an opening day shutout for Cleveland on March 31 against Anaheim and also blanked the White Sox on May 31. After being traded to the Expos on June 27, he threw their only complete-game shutout on August 19 against San Diego.

Carlos Delgado's milestone homers came in an unusual pattern. Delgado's first major league homer came on April 4, 1994 at Toronto's Skydome and was the only home run he hit in that game. His 100th career home run was the first of two homers he smashed at Tiger Stadium on September 17, 1998. Delgado capped a three-homer game on April 20, 2001, at Kansas City's Kauffman Stadium with his 200th career homer. At Skydome on September 25, 2003, Delgado became just the 15th player to hit four home runs in a single game, the first of which was the 300th of his career.

Baseball's all-time home run king Hank Aaron hit his first homer against Cardinals' hurler Vic Raschi on April 23, 1954, in the sixth inning at Sportsman's Park in St. Louis. Braves' catcher Charlie White also hit his first career homer for the Braves in the 14th inning of Milwaukee's 7-5 win. Aaron would hit another 754 homers, but White never hit another one in his brief big league career.

On December 11, 1986, the Mets and Padres pulled off an unusual trade – an eight-player trade involving four players named "Kevin". New York acquired Kevin McReynolds, pitcher Gene Walter, and Adam Ging, a minor league infielder. In exchange San Diego received Kevin Mitchell, Shawn Abner, Stanley Jefferson, and minor league pitchers Kevin Brown and Kevin Armstrong.

Tino Martinez hit his 300th career home run a very long way from his home ballpark. The Devil Rays and Yankees opened the 2004 season with a two-game series in Tokyo, Japan. Martinez, playing in his first game for Tampa Bay, belted his milestone four-bagger against Yankees' pitcher Felix Heredia in the seventh inning of the first game on March 30.

During the 2002 season, Eddie Perez collected four RBIs in 42 games and 117 at-bats for the Cleveland Indians. On opening day, April 5, Perez got three RBIs by smacking a bases-loaded double against Detroit's Mark Redman at Comerica Park in his first at-bat of the year. His last RBI did not come until his 114th at-bat on September 27 at Jacobs Field (the next-to-last day of the season) when he scored Lee Stevens with a double to deep center against Kansas City's Wes Obermueller.

Goose Gossage career spanned the player strikes of 1972, 1981, and ended with the strike of 1994. On the other hand, Ryne Sandberg was not involved the player strikes of 1981 and 1994 because he made his debut on September 2, 1981, after the 1981 strike ended, and then retired in June 1994, before the 1994 strike began in August. Following the shortened 1995 season, Sandberg came out of retirement to rejoin the Cubs for the 1996 and 1997 seasons.

In two official at-bats, pitcher Esteban Yan has swung at only two pitches – *and has two hits.* During an interleague game on June 4, 2000, at Shea Stadium, Yan homered for Tampa Bay against Bobby Jones on the first pitch of his first career at-bat. Yan did not bat again until June 30, 2003, when he was in the NL with the Cardinals. Trailing the Giants 5-0, the Cardinals allowed Yan to bat against Jason Schmidt with two outs in the bottom of the eighth. After taking the first pitch for a ball, Yan bunted the next pitch to second base and beat out an infield hit.

Anaheim Angel pitcher Brendan Donnelly was the winning pitcher of both a World Series game and an All-Star Game – *before he won his second regular season game.* Donnelly's first career regular season win came in his rookie year on September 12, 2002. He gave up a game-tying homer in the top of the ninth against Oakland's Eric Chavez but was the winner when the Angels rallied to win in the bottom of the ninth. Donnelly's next win was as a World Series pitcher in Game 6 of the 2002 Fall Classic. Following the Angels' three-run rally in the bottom of the seventh to cut the Giants' lead to 5-3, he entered the game and shut down the Giants in the eighth (striking out two) and was the winner when the Angels plated three more in the bottom of the eighth. Donnelly's third win was in the 2003 All-Star Game in Chicago when he pitched a perfect eighth inning and the AL rallied to beat the NL on Hank Blalock's home run against Eric Gagne in the bottom of the frame. Donnelly's second regular season win was not until July 28, 2003, when he pitched one inning of scoreless relief at Oakland.

On May 31, 1988, New York Yankees' pitcher Neil Allen pitched a nine-inning shutout against Oakland – *but did not get credit for a complete game.* Al Leiter, the Yankees' rookie starting pitcher, was injured on his first pitch of the game when he was hit in the forearm by Carney Lansford's line drive. Leiter picked up the ball but threw wildly to first base, allowing Lansford to reach second. Allen replaced the injured Leiter and retired the first 19 batters he faced on the way to a 5-0 win.

Phil Cavarretta ended his 20-year stay with the Chicago Cubs after the 1953 season having appeared in 1,953 games for the team.

When the Tampa Bay Devil Rays entered major league baseball for the 1998 season, the American League East standings finished in identical order for the next seven seasons. The Yankees won the division title each season followed by the Red Sox, Blue Jays, Orioles, and Devil Rays. The streak ended in 2004 when the Blue Jays fell from third to last.

In the sixth inning of a game against Oakland on June 26, 1992, Minnesota catcher Brian Harper's hustle resulted in a very unusual putout. Mike Bordick lined a shot off the foot of Twins' pitcher Willie Banks and the ball deflected into foul territory along the first baseline. Harper, running to back up first base, snared the ball with his bare hand and, as he dove headfirst, fired to the bag for a 1-2-3 putout of Bordick.

Steve Garvey had six 200-hit seasons, but because he did not draw many walks (just 479 in 2,332 games) or steal many bases (83 in 145 attempts), he never scored 100 runs in a season. Doc Cramer is the only other player to have even three 200-hit seasons (1934, 1935, and 1940) without scoring 100 runs in at least one of them, although he did score 100 runs in three other years (1933, 1938, and 1939) when he had fewer than 200 hits.

Vinny Castilla grounded into *exactly* 22 double plays each season from 2001 to 2004.

An injury prevented the Rockies' catcher Brent Mayne from swinging a bat, but – *despite never pitching at any level of baseball in his career* – he was called on to pitch against the Atlanta Braves when Colorado ran out of pitchers on August 22, 2000, at Coors Field. Mayne entered the game as the 10th Rockie pitcher in the 12th inning with the score tied at 6-6. Pitcher Tom Glavine, batting because the Braves were out of position players, was the first hitter and grounded back to Mayne. Walt Weiss followed with a fly ball to center. Following a single up the middle by Rafael Furcal, Mayne walked Andruw Jones. The next batter was Chipper Jones who ended the inning by grounding to third on a check-swing. With the bases loaded and two outs in the bottom of the 12th, Mayne's spot in the batting order was due at the plate. Because Mayne was unable to hit, Adam Melhuse pinch-hit for him and singled to left – *for his first major league hit* – to win the game 7-6. Mayne is the last non-pitcher to win a game.

In 1,155 big league games, free-swinging slugger Rob Deer reached base by hit or walk 1,428 times (853 hits and 575 walks) – barely more than his 1,409 career strikeouts. Deer's hit total is 420 lower than that of Jay Buhner, the next closest player who stuck out 1,400 times.

Josh Hancock's first big league win was for the Cincinnati Reds – *although he was not a member of the team when the game began.* Rain delays plagued the Cincinnati-Houston game on July 30, 2004, but solo homers by Adam Dunn and Felipe Lopez off Pete Munro had the Reds in front 2-1 in the fifth inning. Just as heavy rain returned, Jeff Bagwell singled to center to tie the game and then the umpires were forced to delay the action a third time and eventually suspend the game for the night. During the final delay the Reds finalized a trade with the Phillies to acquire Hancock for pitcher Todd Jones. Hancock arrived the next day as the suspended game was resuming before the regularly scheduled game. He entered the game in the top of the 13th and ended up the winner when the Reds scored on a walk to Wily Mo Pena and a double by Jason LaRue.

Since 1983 only three National League batting champions have come from teams east of the Mississippi River. Montreal's Tim Raines won with a .336 average in 1986, Atlanta's Terry Pendleton topped the NL with a .319 mark in 1991, and Chicago's Derek Lee took the 2005 batting crown with a .335 average. The other 19 NL batting titles were won by Tony Gwynn (8) and Gary Sheffield (1) of San Diego, Larry Walker (3), Andres Galarraga (1) and Todd Helton (1) of Colorado, Willie McGee (2) and Albert Pujols (1) of St. Louis and Barry Bonds (2) of San Francisco.

When St. Louis took on Houston at the Astrodome on June 2, 1986, starting pitcher John Tudor pitched a complete game, and the Cardinals made no defensive substitutions and did not use a pinch hitter or a pinch runner. Each of the nine Cardinals that played scored *exactly* one run as St. Louis won 9-2.

Otis Nixon hit just 11 home runs in 5,115 at-bats during his career from 1983 to 1999, but he managed to spread them out among six different teams – Cleveland (3), Montreal (1), Atlanta (3), Toronto (2), Los Angeles (1), and Minnesota (1). Two of Nixon's three homers with the Braves came against the same pitcher within the span of one week in 1992. He connected against Trevor Wilson on June 24 at Atlanta and on June 30 at San Francisco.

New York's Gene Woodling hit three homers off Cleveland's Early Wynn in 1951. Each was a two-run homer, and they came on June 24, July 24 and August 24.

Tony Perez had two seasons in which he collected exactly 32 doubles, six triples, and 19 home runs while driving in 91 runs – *and he did it in back-to-back seasons with different teams.* Perez posted those totals in 1976 with the Cincinnati Reds and matched them the next season following his trade to the Montreal Expos.

During the 7-5 win over the Royals on July 26, 1990, the Blue Jays scored three runs *on a strikeout.* With the bases loaded and two outs in the second, Mookie Wilson swung at a 3-2 pitch that bounced in the dirt and rolled just a few feet away. Royals' catcher Mike Macfarlane picked up the ball and, rather than step on the plate for a force play, threw wildly to first, which allowed three runs to score.

The first *four* times that Seattle pitcher Freddy Garcia faced the Detroit Tigers he did it in a different ballpark. As a rookie in 1999, he beat them three times – April 28 at the Kingdome, June 17 at Tiger Stadium, and August 24 at Safeco Field. On April 11, 2000, in his second start of the next season, the Tigers beat him at Comerica Park.

The A's entered their August 24, 2003, game at Toronto without a grand slam in the first 129 games of the season – *then hit two grand slams in a game for the first time in the 103-year history of the franchise.* Ramon Hernandez gave Oakland a quick 4-0 lead in the first when he connected against Kelvim Escobar. Miguel Tejada's sixth-inning slam against Josh Towers made the score 12-2 as Oakland went on to win 17-2.

Mickey Tettleton retired on July 6, 1997, after a knee injury limited him to only four hits in 44 at-bats for the Texas Rangers during the first half of the 1997 season. His four hits included his last three home runs – *which were all solo homers and came in consecutive games.* During the final two games of a series with Baltimore at The Ballpark in Arlington, Tettleton homered on April 5 against Arthur Rhodes and on April 6 against Mike Johnson and then went deep the next day at Milwaukee's County Stadium against Jose Mercedes. His last hit was a double off Angels' pitcher Shigetoshi Hasegawa on June 23.

On July 17, 2004, Greg Maddux notched his 297th win and his last career shutout (as of the 2005 season) by holding Milwaukee to six hits and beating them 5-0 at Wrigley Field. The victory was his first complete game since July 17, 2003, and his first shutout since he beat Tampa Bay 4-0 on July 17, 2001.

Rick Wrona got five hits in ten at-bats in his last big league season – *all five were extra-base hits and three of them came in his last game.* As a member of the 1994 Milwaukee Brewers, Wrona hit a homer against the Twins' Mike Trombley in the seventh inning at the Metrodome on July 17 for his first extra-base hit since his home run for the Cubs at St. Louis on October 1, 1989. Three days after his homer, he batted once against Kansas City and doubled against Stan Belinda. Wrona banged out the last of his 41 big league hits by going 3 for 4 against the Twins on July 22 at County Stadium with each hit being a double against a different pitcher. He did not appear in another game before the players' strike ended the 1994 season on August 10 and was not picked up for the 1995 season. He finished his career with just ten extra-base hits in 168 at-bats.

Fred Mitchell played for six teams – but in just three cities. Mitchell spent time with the Boston Red Sox (1901-1902) and the Boston Brave (1913), the Philadelphia A's (1902) and the Philadelphia Phillies (1903-1904), and the Brooklyn Dodgers (1904-1905) and New York Yankees (1910). He is the only player to play for two teams in three different cities.

During his first year in the NL with the San Francisco Giants, Billy Pierce started 12 games at Candlestick Park in 1962 and was 12-0. In his home starts Pierce compiled an ERA of 2.69 with 44 strikeouts in 97 innings, beating Chicago three times, Cincinnati, St. Louis, Philadelphia and Los Angeles twice each, and Houston once. The closest he came to losing at home was on May 25 when he was roughed up for seven earned runs in 8.1 innings but received ten runs of support from his teammates. Pierce started 11 games on the road and was 3-6 with a 4.90 ERA and 25 strikeouts in 60.2 innings. He also pitched seven games in relief and finished the season 16-6 with a 3.50 ERA and 76 strikeouts.

Mike Bordick finished his 14-year career in 2003 with some nice round numbers – exactly 1,500 hits, exactly 800 strikeouts and exactly 500 walks.

Cal Ripken, Jr.'s first major league stolen base was a steal of home as part of a double steal in the sixth inning of his 67th major league game on May 31, 1982, against the Texas Rangers. Ripken played another 2,934 games but never stole home again.

The last game of Todd Fischer's brief nine-game pitching career was on July 10, 1986, *when he balked in the winning run without throwing a pitch.* The Angels lead the Red Sox 7-4 entering the bottom of the twelfth only to see Boston rally to tie the game behind a two-run homer from Jim Rice followed by an error, a walk, and a single by Rich Gedman. Fischer entered the game with the bases loaded and Rey Quinones at the plate. Before the first pitch home plate umpire Joe Brinkman called a balk as Fischer removed his hand from his glove during his stretch, allowing Dwight Evans to score with the winning run from third base.

Ken Griffey, Jr. played 17 seasons before he ended a season with a home run total in the 30s. Starting in his rookie year of 1989 at age 19, Griffey's highest single-season total during his first four years was 27 in 1992. Beginning the next season, Griffey hit at least 40 homers in seven of the next eight years (including back-to-back years of 56), with a broken hand limiting him to 17 homers in 72 games in 1995. From 2001 to 2004, injuries again took their toll and held him to a total of 63 homers in 317 games. Healthy again in 2005, Griffey was on pace for another 40-homer year when he injured his right foot on September 4, ending his season at 35 homers.

From 1965 to 1973, Jim Hickman had 22 stolen base attempts. He was successful 13 time and caught stealing nine times – *exactly one time each season.*

In Boston's 29-4 win over the St. Louis Browns at Fenway Park on June 8, 1950, Al Zarilla was 5 for 7, including a record-tying four doubles – *but did not drive in a single run.* With the game scoreless, Zarilla doubled to right to start the second. The Red Sox batted around and, following a homer by Walt Dropo, Zarilla came to the plate again and doubled to center. In the next inning, he collected another two-bagger with Dropo going from first to third on the hit.

After popping to shortstop in the fourth, Zarilla got his last double in the fifth inning by going to right field, but again Dropo was stopped at third base. Zarilla singled to begin the seventh and ended his day by flying out in the eighth. The offensive barrage featured big games by Bobby Doerr (3 homers, 8 RBIs), Walt Dropo, (2 homers, 7 RBIs), and Ted Williams, (2 homers, 5 RBIs) and resulted in the most lopsided game in big league history. Boston starting pitcher Chuck Stobbs pitched a complete game plus walked in four consecutive plate appearances to go with two singles and an RBI. Coupled with their 20-4 win over St. Louis the day before, the Red Sox set a record with 49 runs in consecutive games.

Leo Cardenas played in 150 games and batted 551 times for the California Angels in 1972 but scored just 25 runs. No other player has batted at least 500 times and scored less often.

In the second inning of the Mariners' 5-4 interleague win over the Pirates on June 18, 2004, Seattle pitcher Jamie Moyer collected a bases-loaded single over third base against Ryan Vogelsong that scored Scott Spiezio and Dan Wilson. These were his first RBIs since he drew a bases-loaded walk against Montreal's Floyd Youmans on April 8, 1988, when he was with the Chicago Cubs. No player has ever had a longer stretch between RBIs.

During a July 23, 2002, day-night doubleheader at Fenway Park, the Boston Red Sox scored 26 unanswered runs against Tampa Bay – *but did not sweep them*. After spotting the Devil Rays two runs in each of the first two innings, Boston erupted for ten runs in the third, highlighted by two homers from Nomar Garciaparra. They plated six more in the third (including a Garciaparra grand slam against Brandon Backe) and tacked on six more runs later to win 22-4. Garciaparra's big night was on his 29th birthday, making him the only player to celebrate his birthday with a three-homer game. In the second game, Boston jumped to a quick lead in the second game with two in the first and two more in the fourth and led 4-0 heading into the ninth. In the top of the ninth, *after being held scoreless for 15 straight innings*, Tampa Bay broke out for five runs, capped by a three-run homer from Jared Sandberg against Ugueth Urbina. The Devil Rays held on to win 5-4, ending a ten-game losing steak against Boston.

Over a three-year span, Tony Clark scored 113 run – *almost 55 percent of them by driving himself in with a home run.* Clark hit 16 homers and scored just 29 times for the Mets in 2003 and followed that with 16 homers and 37 runs for the Yankees in 2004. The next season Clark was with the Diamondbacks and hit 30 homers but scored just 47 runs, nine runs worse than the next lowest total for a player with a 30-homer season.

After spending 13 years with the Chicago Cubs in the National League, Sammy Sosa joined the AL's Baltimore Orioles in 2005 and homered at Fenway Park on June 1 for his 579th career homer – *and his first homer at Fenway since his first career home run on June 21, 1989.* The 5,824-day span between Sosa's home runs broke the record for length of time between homers in a ballpark, topping Luke Appling who went 5,810 days (June 4, 1933, to May 1, 1949) between homers at Sportsman's Park in St. Louis. Appling, however, came nowhere close to hitting as many home runs in between as Sosa did – he hit just 45 homers for his career with his two at Sportsman's Park being his seventh and 42nd.

Philadelphia's Randy Wolf pitched a one-hitter against the Cincinnati Reds on September 26, 2001, allowing only a first inning line drive single to Raul Gonzalez – the first career hit for the 27-year-old Gonzalez.

One and Only

Reggie Sanders is the only player to play a complete season with a different team for seven straight years. Following eight seasons with the Cincinnati Reds, Sanders left after the 1998 season and then spent one year with San Diego, Atlanta, Arizona, San Francisco, Pittsburgh, and St. Louis. In 2005 he ended his streak by staying for a second year with St. Louis. During his journey, Sanders was in the right place at the right time to play in the World Series with Arizona (2001), San Francisco (2002) and St. Louis (2004).

Manuel Lee is the only player to strike out more than 100 times in a season without hitting a home run. Lee batted .234 in 445 at-bats for the 1991 Toronto Blue Jays and fanned 107 times without homering.

Reggie Jackson is the only slugger to win home run championships with three different teams. Jackson led the AL with 32 homers in 1973 and 36 more in 1975 while playing for the Oakland A's. He also led the AL with 41 homers in 1980 when he was with the New York Yankees and with 39 homers in 1982 when he played for the California Angels.

On July 17, 1990, the Minnesota Twins made baseball history by turning two triple plays in one game, pulling off the feat at Fenway Park against the Red Sox in the fourth and eighth innings. Both triple plays began with a ground ball to Twin third baseman Gary Gaetti who threw to second baseman Al Newman who then relayed to first baseman Kent Hrbek. The next night Minnesota had six double plays and Boston added four more as the two clubs set another major league record by combining for ten double plays in a single game.

Rod Carew is the only American League player to win the batting title without hitting a home run. Carew batted a league-leading .318 for the Minnesota Twins but did not homer in 1972 – the *only* season in his 19-year career in which he failed to homer. Carew is also the only player with 3,000 hits who finished with fewer than 4,000 total bases. He ended his career with 3,053 hits – 2,404 singles, 445 doubles, 112 triples, and 92 home runs – for 3,998 total bases.

The 1984 Chicago Cubs are the only team to have six players with 80 or more RBIs and yet have nobody with 100 RBIs. Ron Cey led the team with 97 RBIs, followed by Leon Durham (96), Jody Davis (94), Ryne Sandberg (84), Gary Matthews (82), and Keith Moreland (80).

The 1930 St. Louis Cardinals are the only team from the National League to score 1,000 runs in a season. They had three players top the 100-run mark and three others break 90 as they scored 1,004 times. Led by Kiki Cuyler (155 runs), Woody English (152), and Hack Wilson (146), the 1930 Chicago Cubs came very close to joining the Cardinals. They scored 13 runs in each of their last two games but still finished just short with 998 runs.

Lance Johnson finished in the top ten in the league in hits only *two times* in his career, but he is the only player to lead both the NL and AL in hits – *and he did it in consecutive seasons.* After Johnson led the AL in both hits (186) and at-bats (607) for the Chicago White Sox in 1995, he signed with the Mets as a free agent and promptly led the NL in both categories in 1996, this time with 227 hits in 682 at-bats. Johnson is still the only player in Mets' history to have a 200-hit season.

Vida Blue is the only pitcher with a 300-strikeout season who never struck out 200 batters in any other season. Blue whiffed 301 batters with the 1971 Oakland A's, but his next-best total was in 1975 when he struck out just 189.

Dave Kingman is the only player to hit 30 or more homers in his last season. Kingman finished his 16-year career in 1986 with the Oakland A's, hitting just .210 (118 for 561) but walloping 35 homers.

John Valentin is the only player to perform each of these achievements – perform an unassisted triple play (July 8, 1994), hit three homers in a game (June 2, 1995), and hit for the cycle (June 6, 1996).

The 2001 Milwaukee Brewers are the only team to have more strikeouts than hits. They knocked out 1,378 hits, but also struck out a record 1,399 times. Jose Hernandez led the team with 185 strikeouts, followed by Richie Sexson (178) and Jeromy Burnitz (150).

The 1972 New York Mets are the only team since 1900 that did not have a player collect at least 100 hits. The Mets played just 156 games that season because a player's strike delayed the start of the season and resulted in every club losing some games. Tommie Agee led the team with 96 hits, followed by Cleon Jones with 92 and Bud Harrelson with 90.

Bob Friend is the only pitcher whose career began after 1900 to lose at least 200 games while winning fewer than 200 times. During his 16-year career from 1951 to 1966, Friend won 197 and lost 230.

Barry Bonds is the only player to win more than two consecutive MVP Awards – claiming the trophy *four* consecutive times from 2001 to 2004. Stan Musial, Mickey Mantle and Yogi Berra each came close to three consecutive MVP awards. Musial won the NL MVP in 1948 and finished second each of the next three years. Mantle finished second to teammate Roger Maris in both 1960 (by three points) and in 1961 (by four points) before winning the award in 1962. Berra won consecutive MVPs for the New York Yankees in 1954 and 1955, between second-place finishes in 1953 and 1956. Bonds came close to winning four straight MVP Awards a full decade earlier – he claimed his first MVP in 1990, finished second to Terry Pendleton in 1991 by only 15 points, and then won again in 1992 and 1993.

Johnny Mize is the only player with a 50-homer season who had more homers than strikeouts. In 1947 with the New York Giants, Mize hit 52 homers and fanned just 42 times in 586 at-bats.

Chuck Aleno's career consisted of 320 at-bats from 1941 to 1944. Aleno hit just two home runs, but his last one was a fifth-inning clout against Jim Tobin on May 15, 1944, at Crosley Field that accounted for the lone run in Clyde Shoun's 1-0 no-hitter against the Boston Braves. Shoun missed a perfect game by allowing just one walk – *to the opposing pitcher Tobin in the fifth inning.*

Kirk Gibson had a two-homer game on each of his last two birthdays while he was a major league player. Celebrating his 37th birthday on May 28, 1994, at Minnesota's Metrodome, Gibson pinch-hit for Danny Bautista in the seventh and hit a three-run homer off Carl Willis. He stayed in the game at center field and hit a solo shot off Mark Guthrie in the ninth. One year later at Tiger Stadium, the Tigers and White Sox set a major league record by hitting 12 home runs with Gibson connecting for solo homers off Kirk McCaskill in the fourth and Rob Dibble in the sixth. Gibson hit just one more homer before playing in his final major league game on August 10, 1995.

Colorado's Todd Helton is the only hitter to get 100 extra-base hits in consecutive years. Helton had 103 in 2000 (59 doubles, two triples, 42 homers) and followed that with 105 (54 doubles, two triples, 49 homers) in 2001.

Joe Carter is the only player to have three consecutive 100-RBI seasons while playing with three different teams. Carter drove in 105 runs for the 1989 Cleveland Indians, 115 runs for the 1990 San Diego Padres, and 108 runs for the 1991 Toronto Blue Jays.

Mike Mussina and Kevin Brown are the only teammates to collect their 200th career win in the same season – *and they did it in consecutive games.* On April 11, 2004, Mussina won his 200th (on his fifth try), giving up seven hits and three earned runs in 6.1 innings as New York beat the White Sox 5-4 at Yankee Stadium. Following an off-day and a rainout, Brown raised his record to 3-0 as he beat the Devil Rays 5-1. It was Brown's third win as a Yankee, all three against Tampa Bay and each in a different stadium. He beat them at the Tokyo Dome on March 31 during the Yankees' season-opening series, beat them on April 7 at Tampa Bay and then got his 200th win at Yankee Stadium on April 14. In each of the three games, Brown pitched seven innings and allowed one earned run. On September 28, 2003, the last day of the previous season, the Yankees' David Wells won his 200th career game by throwing 7.2 innings of four-hit ball, beating Baltimore 3-1. Wells' win, when combined with those by Mussina and Brown, means that within the span of ten regular season games (only five of which were at home) and six team victories, three New York pitchers won their 200th game at Yankee Stadium.

Ron LeFlore is the only player to lead each league in stolen bases. LeFlore led the AL with 68 steals in 1978 with Detroit and topped the NL by swiping 97 bases, in his only National League season, with Montreal in 1980.

Colorado's Ben Petrick set a record by driving in four runs in a game *in which he did not get a hit.* On September 20, 2000, San Diego beat the Rockies 15-11 at Coors Field and Petrick was 0 for 3 but still had a productive game by driving in four runs. Three times he knocked in Todd Hollandsworth, the first time with a ground ball to shortstop in the second, then with a sacrifice fly to center in the fourth, and finally with a grounder to second base in the eighth. In the ninth inning Petrick drew a bases-loaded walk which scored Todd Walker.

Juan Gonzalez is the only player to have a season in which he averaged an RBI per game (minimum 100 RBIs) with two different clubs. Gonzalez drove in 144 in 134 games in 1996 and 157 in 154 games in 1998, both years with Texas, and had 140 RBIs in 140 games for Cleveland in 2001.

Due to the fact that he walked 2,190 times in his career, Rickey Henderson is the only player with more than 3,000 hits to play in more games than he had hits. He got 3,055 base hits in 3,081 games.

Dan Miceli is the only pitcher to pitch for teams in four divisions in the same season. Miceli began the 2003 season with the Colorado Rockies and was 0-2 in 14 appearances before being released on May 13 and signing with the Cleveland Indians for whom he pitched in 13 games and was 1-1. Sent to the New York Yankees for future considerations on June 25, Miceli did not get a decision with the Yankees in seven games. New York sent him to Houston on July 29 (again for future considerations) where he was 1-1 in 23 games with the Astros.

Entering the game against the Red Sox on July 29, 2003, the Rangers' pitching staff had not allowed a grand slam during the entire season but then allowed Bill Mueller to hit one from *each side of the plate*, making him the only player to do it in one game. In a 14-7 rout of the Rangers, Mueller connected for a solo homer (batting lefthanded) against R.A. Dickey in the third. In the seventh he batted righthanded and hit a slam off Aaron Fultz and followed an inning later with a lefthanded slam off Jay Powell. It was his first three-homer game and gave him a career high nine RBIs.

Rusty Staub is the only player to collect at least 500 hits with four teams. Staub had 792 hits with Houston, 709 with the New York Mets, 582 with Detroit, and 531 with Montreal. He also collected 102 for Texas to give him a career total of 2,716 base hits.

Cecil Fielder hit five home runs against the Oakland A's in 1996 – *and they came in four different ballparks*. The A's began the season by playing six games at Cashman Field in Las Vegas while their ballpark in Oakland was undergoing renovations. Fielder and the Detroit Tigers played four of those games, and the big slugger homered against Carlos Reyes with two outs in the fifth of the game on April 6. Back at Tiger Stadium on April 28, Fielder hit a two-run shot with two outs in the first against Steve Wojciechowski. On June 25 at Oakland's Alameda County Stadium, he led off the seventh with a dinger against Steve Montgomery. Fielder was dealt to the New York Yankees on July 31, which allowed him to face the A's at Yankee Stadium where he homered against Doug Johns on August 23. He later added another four-bagger against the A's at Oakland on September 2 against Buddy Groom .

Only one player has led the league in homers or RBIs while splitting the season with two teams. After driving in four runs in only four games with the 1951 Chicago White Sox, Gus Zernial was traded to the Philadelphia Athletics and went on to compile league-leading totals of 33 homers and 129 RBIs.

The much-traveled Bobo Newsom is the only pitcher since 1900 to win 200 games and still finish his career with a losing record. Newsom was 211-222 with a 3.98 ERA in 600 games. He also had a record five stints with one team. Newsom was with the Washington Senators for part of 1935, 1936, and part of 1937, returned for part of 1942, was traded again, and then reacquired for part of 1943. Later, he was brought back for parts of the 1946 and 1947 seasons and then reacquired yet again in 1952. Newsom also played for the Brooklyn Dodgers (twice), Chicago Cubs, St. Louis Browns (three times), Boston Red Sox, Detroit Tigers, Philadelphia A's (twice), New York Yankees, and New York Giants.

Jay Buhner is the only player to end his career with 300 home runs but drive in fewer than 1,000 runs, finishing his 15-year career in 2001 with 310 homers and 965 RBIs. Darryl Strawberry came very close – he ended up with 335 homers and drove in exactly 1,000 runs.

Mariano Rivera and Jeff Montgomery are the only pitchers with 300 saves to get them all with one team. Rivera has 379 saves with the Yankees through the 2005 season. Montgomery retired from the Kansas City Royals following the 1999 season with 304 saves.

George Mullin is the only pitcher to lose 20 games for a team that won the pennant. Mullin compiled a 20-20 record and a 2.59 ERA for the 1907 Detroit Tigers team that won the AL pennant with a 92-58 record. He started 42 times in 46 appearances, throwing 35 complete games and 357.1 total innings.

Miguel Dilone is the only player to steal 50 or more bases without hitting a triple. Dilone appeared in 135 games for Oakland in 1978 but batted just 258 times, collecting 59 hits and stealing 50 bases. He scored just 34 runs, also the fewest by a player with at least 50 steals.

Tommy Davis is the only player to drive in 150 or more runs in a season *and never have another 100-RBI season.* Davis hit a career-high 27 homers as he knocked in 153 runs for the 1962 Los Angeles Dodgers, but his next best RBI total was just 89, which he did in 1969 when he split time between Seattle and Houston and again in 1973 with Baltimore.

Lou Brock is the only player with 1,500 strikeouts who hit fewer than 200 homers. Brock finished his 19-year career in 1979 with 149 homers and 1,730 strikeouts.

Gary Sheffield is the only player to have a 100-RBI season with five different teams. Sheffield had his first 100-RBI year for the Milwaukee Brewers in 1992 but his next one was not until he drove in 120 runs for the Florida Marlins in 1996. From 1999 to 2001, Sheffield had three consecutive 100-RBI seasons (101, 109, and 100) with the Los Angeles Dodgers. Sheffield set his career high for RBI by driving in 132 for the 2003 Atlanta Braves and followed with 121 RBIs in 2004 and 123 RBIs in 2005 for the New York Yankees.

Albert Pujols is the only player to begin his career with more than three consecutive seasons of 30 homers and 100 RBIs. Pujols won the National League Rookie of the Year award in 2001 with

37 homers and 130 RBIs and has continued his hot hitting through the end of the 2005 season. The Cardinals' slugger compiled similar totals in 2002 (34 homers, 127 RBIs), 2003 (43 and 124), 2004 (46 and 123), and 2005 (41 and 117). During his first five years, Pujols' at-bat totals were amazingly consistent – 590, 590, 591, 592, and 591.

Willie Mays finished his career with 1,526 strikeouts and a batting average of .302, making him the only player to whiff 1,500 times and still have a lifetime average greater than .300.

Phil Cavarretta's major league career was from 1935 to 1955 – making him the *only* player who was active during Babe Ruth's last season (1935) and Hank Aaron's first season (1954).

Darryl Strawberry is the only player to appear in the World Series with both the New York Mets and New York Yankees. Strawberry was a member of the Mets when they beat Boston in the 1986 World Series and was part of the Yankees' 1996 World Series championship over the Atlanta Braves. Strawberry was also a member of the 1998 Yankees but was hospitalized following cancer surgery when New York swept the San Diego Padres in the World Series. He recovered to rejoin the Yankees the following year when they swept the Atlanta Braves in the 1999 World Series. Dwight Gooden, Strawberry's teammate on the 1986 Mets, was also a member of the Yankees in 1996 – and even threw a no-hitter on May 14 – but was left off the playoff roster and did not appear in the 1996 World Series.

George Sisler is the only player to have a 200-hit season and score fewer than 70 runs. He had 205 hits and 67 runs for the 1929 Boston Braves.

Tony Oliva is the only rookie to win a major league batting championship. After only 16 games with the Twins in the 1962 and 1963 seasons, Oliva collected 217 hits while posting a league-high .323 average in 1964. He added another batting title the next year when he hit .321 and won a third batting crown in 1971 when he hit .337.

In the 2004 season, Anaheim's Alfredo Amezaga became the only player since 1900 to hit two grand slams but *no other home runs* in a season. Amezaga hit safely 15 times in 93 at-bats, connecting for grand slams against Mike Myers in the ninth inning of the Angels' 10-7 loss at Fenway Park on August 31 and against Joe Blanton in the sixth inning of a 10-0 win at Oakland on October 1.

Jim Tobin is the only pitcher since 1900 to hit three home runs in one game. On May 13, 1942, Tobin hit solo shots off Jake Mooty in the fifth and seventh innings and broke a 4-4 tie with a two-run homer in the eighth inning against Hi Bithorn, leading the Boston Braves to a 6-5 win over the Cubs at Braves Field.

Sammy Sosa and Rafael Palmeiro are the only 500-home run hitters to be teammates on two different teams in their careers – *but they never homered in the same game.* After three seasons with the Cubs, Palmeiro was traded to Texas for the 1989 season and hit eight homers in 156 games. Sosa began his major league career with the Rangers on June 16, 1989, and hit one homer with them on June 21 before being traded to the Chicago White Sox on July 29. After 13 seasons with the Cubs, Sosa was traded to Baltimore on February 2, 2005, and rejoined Palmeiro who was in his second stint with the Orioles. The pair combined for 32 homers in 2005 (Sosa with 14, Palmerio with 18), but they never homered in the same game and were each let go by Baltimore following the season. When the Orioles played the Reds at the Great American Ballpark in Cincinnati on June 10, 2005, Sosa and Palmeiro were joined on the field by Ken Griffey, Jr. – making it the first time that three players with 500 homers appeared in the same game.

Ron Hassey made baseball history by catching *two perfect games.* Hassey contributed an RBI single while catching Len Barker as the Cleveland righthander retired 27 straight Blue Jays and won 3-0 on May 15, 1981. More than a decade later with Montreal, Hassey was behind the plate for the 2-0 masterpiece thrown by Dennis Martinez against the Dodgers on July 28, 1991.

Fred McGriff is the only player to have *two* 100-RBI seasons while splitting time between two big league clubs. McGriff drove in 101 runs in 1993 while playing for San Diego (46 RBIs) and Atlanta (55) and split his 102 RBIs in 2001 between Tampa Bay (61) and the Chicago Cubs (41).

The 1978 Orioles are the only team since divisional play began in 1969 to win 90 games and finish fourth. They finished 90-71 but still ended up behind New York (100-63), Boston (99-64), and Milwaukee (93-69).

Albert Belle ended his career with nine straight 100-RBI seasons, including 103 in this final season with the 2000 Baltimore Orioles. Despite playing with a painful degenerative hip condition for part of the season and missing 20 games in September, Belle had 97 RBIs entering the last week of the season. He knocked in six runs in the final four games to sneak past the century mark, the last two RBIs coming as the result of a home run in his final major league at-bat against Denny Neagle on October 1. When it became clear in spring training of 2001 that the painful hip would prevent him running effectively, the 34-year-old Belle retired from the game, making him the only player since 1900 to end his career with a 100-RBI season.

Brian Daubach is the only player to have four seasons of at least 20 homers and still finish with fewer than 100 career homers. After beginning his career with ten games for Florida in 1998, Daubach moved over to Boston in 1999 and had home run totals of 21, 21, 22 and 20 over the next four years. Following the 2002 season, he left Boston for Chicago via the free-agent route and slipped to just six home runs (his next highest season total) for the White Sox in 2003. Daubach had 93 career homers when he last appeared in a major league game on July 8, 2005.

Rafael Palmeiro, with 569 home runs through the 2005 season, holds some unique distinctions from the rest of the 500-home run sluggers. Palmeiro never led the league in either homers or RBIs and never hit three homers in one game (despite 34 two-homer games).

Palmeiro also led the AL in 1990 with 191 singles, making him the only one of the group to lead the league in that category.

Wes Stock is the only pitcher to have two perfect seasons with at least five wins. He was 5-0 in 1961 and 7-0 in 1963 for Baltimore.

Cal Hubbard is the only man elected to both the Baseball Hall of Fame and the NFL Hall of Fame. Hubbard played end, tackle and linebacker for Green Bay, Pittsburgh, and New York in the late 1920s and early 1930s and was elected to Canton in 1963. Following his football career, Hubbard served as an American League umpire from 1936 to 1951 and was enshrined in Cooperstown in 1976.

Bill Melton is the only player since the Deadball Era ended in 1919 to win a home run title but not have a 100-RBI season *at any time during his career.* Melton led the AL with 33 homers for the 1971 White Sox while driving in just 86 runs. His career high in RBIs (96) came one season earlier when he hit 33 homers to become the first 30-homer player in White Sox history.

Ned Garver is the only pitcher since 1905 to win 20 games for a team that lost 100 games. Garver threw 24 complete games and a total of 246 innings for the 1951 St. Louis Browns, finishing with a record of 20-12 and a 3.73 ERA for a team that ended with a 52-102 record. Garver also finished his 14-year career with a unique statistical oddity – he had 881 strikeouts and 881 walks.

Mark McGwire followed up his memorable 70-homer season of 1998 by smacking 65 more in 1999. McGwire did it by hitting safely 145 times while driving in 147 runs – making him the only player with a 100-RBI season to have more RBIs than hits.

In the strike-shortened 1995 season, Cleveland's Albert Belle became the only player to hit at least 50 home runs and doubles in the same season. He collected 50 homers and 52 doubles in 546 at-bats.

Opening Day

On April 20, 1939, Boston's Ted Williams made his major league debut on opening day against New York by collecting one hit in three at-bats. In that game Yankees' great Lou Gehrig went hitless in four at-bats while stretching his consecutive game streak to 2,123 games, just seven games before Amyotrophic Lateral Sclerosis (ALS) would finally force him out of the New York lineup. It was the only time that the two Hall of Fame players appeared in a game together.

On April 5, opening day of the 1993 season, Oakland inserted Eric Fox into center field as a late-inning defensive replacement and he came to bat in the bottom of the eighth, smacking a two-out grand slam against Tom Bolton to secure Oakland's 9-4 victory over the Detroit Tigers. It was Fox's only home run of the season and accounted for four of his five RBIs.

Sixto Lezcano cranked three grand slams among his 148 career home runs – *with two of them coming on opening day.* Lezcano opened the 1978 season on April 7 with a seventh inning grand slam against Baltimore's Tim Stoddard and led the Milwaukee Brewers to an 11-3 win at County Stadium. Two years later on April 10, again at County Stadium, Lezcano smacked a two-run homer against Red Sox starter Dennis Eckersley in the fourth inning before smacking a two-out, ninth-inning grand slam against Dick Drago to make the Brewers a 9-5 winner over Boston

Mike Parrott pitched the Seattle Mariners to a win on the opening day of the 1980 season by allowing three earned runs in 6.1 innings. The victory turned out to be the high point of Parrott's season – he pitched just 27 innings with an ERA of 7.28 in 27 games and finished the year 1-16.

Only three players have hit three homers on opening day – *each time on April 4*. George Bell was the first to accomplish the feat when he homered three times against Royals' pitcher Bret Saberhagen in the 1988 opener for Toronto. Exactly six years later, Chicago Cub outfielder Karl "Tuffy" Rhodes began the 1994 season with three home runs (of his career total of 13) at Wrigley Field against New York's Dwight Gooden. Detroit's Dmitri Young joined the group in 2005 when he began the season with three blasts against Kansas City at Comerica Park, the first two against Jose Lima and the last one off Mike MacDougal.

With three one-hitters already to his credit, 21-year-old Bob Feller opened the 1940 season on April 16 by throwing the only opening day no-hitter in big league history. With his parents and sister in attendance, the Cleveland righthander beat the White Sox 1-0 at Comiskey Park, retiring 15 batters in a row from the fourth through the eighth and finishing with eight strikeouts and five walks.

Two of baseball's most beloved and storied ballparks opened on the same day. Fenway Park and Tiger Stadium each opened on April 20, 1912, and in each game the home team won in extra innings. Boston edged New York 7-6 in 11 innings, and Detroit slipped by Cleveland 6-5, also in 11 innings.

Hall of Famer Mel Ott hit his 511th, and final, home run in the first inning of the opening game of the 1946 season. Serving as the Giants' player-manager for the sixth year, Ott began his 21st season with the Giants by homering against Oscar Judd of the Phillies at the Polo Grounds on April 16. He would insert himself into 30 more games in 1946 and four more in 1947, for a total of 34 more at-bats, but would never homer again.

Dwight Evans hit his only leadoff home run of the 1986 season – *on the very first pitch of the season.* Leading off the year's first game on April 7, Evans drilled the first offering from Jack Morris into the center field bleachers at Tiger Stadium, making him the only player to hit a homer on the season's first pitch. Evans' quick start was wasted as Detroit, behind four hits and two homers from Kirk Gibson, rallied for a 6-5 victory over Boston.

Gee Walker led the Tigers to a 4-3 win at Detroit on April 20, 1937, becoming the only player to hit for the cycle on opening day. The Detroit outfielder homered over the left field wall against Cleveland's Mel Harder in the bottom of the second and, with the Tigers trailing 3-2 in the bottom of the fourth, he tripled and scored the tying run on a wild pitch. Walker added a double and single in his next two at-bats to finish the cycle.

Pitching Feats

In his last season, Nolan Ryan's distinguished career ended on September 22, 1993, against the Seattle Mariners at the Kingdome – *without him retiring any of the six batters he faced.* Ryan gave up a leadoff single to Omar Vizquel and then walked the next three batters before Dann Howitt touched him for a grand slam. With a 3-1 count on the next batter, Dave Magadan, Ryan tore ligaments in his pitching elbow and was forced to leave the game. Howitt's homer was the 10th grand slam hit off Ryan in his long career, breaking the record for the most career grand slams allowed by a pitcher. The blast was also the only grand slam of Howitt's career – he would finish his career in 1994 with just five homers and 22 RBIs.

Harry Coveleski had three consecutive 20-win seasons for the Detroit Tigers – *but did not win more than six games in any other season.* Coveleski, the brother of Hall of Famer Stan Coveleski, first gained fame in 1908. He was called up from the minor by the Phillies in late September and beat the New York Giants three times in a five-day span during a tight pennant race, allowing the Chicago Cubs to take the NL flag. After winning just six times in 24 games for Philadelphia the following year, he was traded to the Cincinnati Reds in January 1910 and was just 1-1 in 7 games for the Reds that season. After a stay in the minors, Coveleski resurfaced with the Detroit Tigers in 1914 and enjoyed three fine years, posting records of 22-12, 22-13, and 21-11. In 1916 he dropped to 4-6 in 16 games and then lost once without winning a game in his final season of 1918, finishing with a career mark of 81-55.

Johnny Humphries pitched the first four of his nine career shutouts for the White Sox in 1941 – *the only four wins he had in 14 games that season.* Humphries won his first game for the White Sox on August 14 with a 3-0 blanking of the Tigers in which he also had an RBI double and scored a run. He gave up six hits and preserved the shutout by stranding seven Tigers in the final three innings. In his next start on August 20, Humphries limited the A's to four hits and won 1-0. He then extended his scoreless steak to 33 innings in his next start with a 3-0 whitewash of the Red Sox in which he drove in two runs with a bases-loaded double. Humphries' last win on the year was a four-hit, 2-0 outing against the Athletics on September 12 at Philadelphia.

Twenty strikeouts in a nine-inning game has been accomplished four times by a total of three pitchers – Roger Clemens (April 29, 1986, and September 18, 1996), Kerry Wood (May 6, 1998), and Randy Johnson (May 8, 2001). Not only did they each strike out 20 batters – *they each did it without issuing a single walk.*

Over five consecutive starts in 1999, Arizona's Randy Johnson allowed just five earned runs and struck out 62 batters in 40 innings – *but was 0-4 in those games.* Johnson began the streak by fanning 14 Cardinals on June 25 but lost 1-0 to Jose Jimenez's no-hitter. The big lefthander pitched well again on June 30, whiffing 17 Reds at Cincinnati in an eight-inning complete game and still lost 2-0. In his next start on July 5, Johnson struck out 12 Cardinals at St. Louis yet again lost to Jimenez by a 1-0 score. Johnson's 43 strikeouts in this three-game stretch tied Dwight Gooden's NL record for most strikeouts in three consecutive games. Johnson made his next start on July 10 against Oakland but lost again despite giving up just one earned run on three hits and racking up 11 strikeouts in seven innings. The next time out on July 15, he got a no-decision despite pitching eight scoreless innings and fanning eight at Texas. Johnson finally got a much-deserved win on July 20 at Seattle when he pitched a complete-game shutout and fanned ten.

Gaylord Perry is the only pitcher since 1918 to post an ERA under 2.00 and lose at least 16 games. Perry won the American League Cy Young Award for the Cleveland Indians in 1972 with a 24-16 record, which included a 1.92 ERA, 234 strikeouts, and 29 complete games.

On July 12, 1997, *in his first appearance against his former team the Boston Red Sox*, Roger Clemens set the Toronto Blue Jays strikeout record by fanning 16 batters at Fenway Park. Clemens notched the 16 strikeouts in only eight innings as Toronto beat Boston 3-1. On August 25, 1998, Clemens would increase the Blue Jays strikeout record by fanning 18 members of the Kansas City Royals.

Tommy John won more than 80 games with three different teams. John won 82 games for the Chicago White Sox (1963-1971), 87 for the Los Angeles Dodgers (1972-1978), and 91 for the New York Yankees (1979-1982, 1986-1989). He also won two games for Cleveland in 1964, 24 games for California (1982-1985) and two games for Oakland in 1985 to finish his career with a total of 288 wins.

Entering the last two weeks of the 2001 season, Roger Clemens had a record of 20-1 with the lone loss coming on May 20 to the Seattle Mariners, who won a record-tying 116 games in 2001. Two of Clemens' final three starts were against the lowly Tampa Bay Devil Rays, the worst team in the AL with a record of 62-100. However, the Devil Rays beat him 4-0 at Yankee Stadium and 8-4 at Tropicana Field to make his final record 20-3.

Ted Gray ended his nine-year career by pitching in a total of 14 games with four different teams in 1955. After appearing in two games for the Chicago White Sox, two games for the Cleveland Indians, and one game for the New York Yankees, Gray finally got a decision by winning once and losing twice in nine appearances for the Baltimore Orioles. He ended his career with a record of 59-74.

New York Met pitcher Anthony Young set a major league record by losing 27 straight decisions. Young got off to a strong start in 1992 by pitching a complete game at St. Louis in his first start of the year, giving up just one unearned run, and then he beat Montreal in relief on April 19 to make his record 2-0. Back in the starting rotation, Young lost three straight beginning May 6 and then four in a row in June before being sent to the bullpen – where he promptly lost twice in his first three appearances. Pitching exclusively in relief, Young saved ten games in his next 23 appearances before taking the loss in five blown saves in September to finish the 1992 season with a 2-14 record. Young started the 1993 season with a blown save loss in his first game and lost three others out of the bullpen before being moved back into the Mets' starting rotation. After a no-decision in his first start, he lost six consecutive outings before being banished to the bullpen again where he lost his 27th consecutive decision on July 24 when the Dodgers rallied against him in the bottom of the 10th. In his next game on July 28, Young allowed an unearned run to Florida in the top of the 9th and seemed destined to lose again, but the Mets rallied for two in the home half of the ninth to beat Florida 5-4 to make him the winning pitcher. During his losing streak, Young had a 6.32 ERA in 98.2 innings and lost to every NL team except Atlanta and the two 1993 expansion teams (Colorado and Florida). Montreal had the most success against Young, beating him five times.

In 1972 Philadelphia's Steve Carlton finished with a record of 27-10, 310 strikeouts and an ERA of 1.97. The Phillies finished the season at 59-97, meaning that Carlton accounted for 45.8 percent of the Phillies wins that year.

Minnesota pitcher Terry Felton holds the dubious major league records for the most single-season losses *and* the most career losses by a pitcher who *never* won a major league game. Felton appeared in seven games with the Twins from 1979 to 1981 and lost three games, all in 1980. In 1982 Felton appeared in 48 games for the Twins and was 0-13 with an ERA of 4.99. On September 12, 1982, Felton relieved Brad Havens with two outs in the fourth. Minnesota led 7-4 after the fourth and Felton could have claimed his first win, but he could not hold the lead. Leading 7-6 in the sixth, Felton was replaced when he issued one-out walks to Willie Wilson and U. L. Washington and ended up with his 13th, and final, loss when the Royals took the lead for good on a single by Amos Otis against Ron Davis later in the inning. Felton's final chance for a major league win was on September 28, 1982, when he was staked to an early 3-0 lead but could not hold it and was replaced after four innings with the score tied. Felton finished his career with a mark of 0-16 and a 5.53 ERA.

Mike Torrez won at least 14 games for five different clubs – *doing it within a five-year span.* Torrez was 15-8 for the 1974 Montreal Expos, followed that with a 20-9 record for Baltimore in 1975, and then had a 16-12 mark for the Oakland A's in 1976. After four games with the A's in 1977, he was traded to New York and was 14-12 for the Yankees in the remainder of the season. Torrez signed with Boston as a free agent for the 1978 season and went 16-13 for the Red Sox.

Don Hankins surrendered just one home run in his brief major league pitching career *–Babe Ruth's only inside-the-park homer in his 60-homer season of 1927.* In the second game of a doubleheader on July 8, Ruth hit his 27th homer of the year into Tiger Stadium's deep center field in the second inning with two men on. Hankins' career ended with a 2-1 record in 42.2 innings, all of them coming for Detroit in the 1927 season.

From his retirement in 1927 until the end of the 1982 season, Walter Johnson was the all-time strikeout leader, but a year later he was bumped down to *fourth* on the list. By the end of the 1983 season, Steve Carlton (3,709), Nolan Ryan (3,677) and Gaylord Perry (3,534) had all passed Johnson's 3,509 career strikeouts.

The Cincinnati Reds and the Atlanta Braves each had a three-year stretch in which they had a different pitcher record 30 or more saves. Cincinnati got 32 saves from John Franco in 1989, 31 from Randy Myers in 1990, and 31 from Rob Dibble in 1991. Atlanta had Mark Wohlers save 33 games in 1997, followed by 30 saves from Kerry Ligtenberg in 1998 and 38 saves from John Rocker in 1999.

Derek Wallace struck out only 20 batters in his career – *but still tied the major league record of four strikeouts in one inning.* As a rookie in 1996, Wallace appeared in 19 games and pitched 24.2 innings for the New York Mets. On September 13 he came into the game in the ninth inning against the Atlanta Braves to protect a 6-4 lead. Wallace struck out Terry Pendleton to lead off the inning, but Pendleton reached first safely on a passed ball. After striking out Chipper Jones, he allowed a double to Fred McGriff but escaped with the save by striking out Ryan Klesko and pinch-hitter Mike Mordecai.

Joe Bush of the 1922 New York Yankees is the only pitcher to win 25 games without throwing a shutout. He pitched in 39 games, starting 30 and completing 20, and compiled a record of 26-7 with a 3.31 ERA in 255.1 innings.

Steve Carlton holds the National League strikeout record with *exactly* 4,000 strikeouts. After seven seasons with the Cardinals, Carlton spent 15 years with the Phillies before they released him on June 24, 1986. He was picked up by the Giants for a brief stint before being released again on August 7. The American League Chicago White Sox gave the great lefthander a chance for the remainder of the 1986 season, and he and hung on in the AL until early 1988, splitting time between Cleveland and Minnesota. In 46 American League games, Carlton whiffed another 136 batters to finish with 4,136 strikeouts.

In their inaugural season of 1993, the Florida Marlins won just 64 games with closer Bryan Harvey playing a significant role in 72 percent of them, saving 45 games and winning one game while posting a 1.70 ERA in 59 appearances.

Don Sutton struck out the most batters (3,574) without ever leading the league and also tied with Nolan Ryan for most career wins (324) by a pitcher who never won a Cy Young Award (awarded since 1956). Sutton also pitched 5,282.1 innings and allowed 472 home runs – the fourth highest total ever – but never hit a home run in his 1,354 at-bats as a hitter.

Bob Welch was 27-6 in 35 starts for the 1990 Oakland A's, pitching a total of 238 innings with just *two* complete games. Steve Stone, with a 25-7 record for Baltimore in 1980, has the next fewest complete games (nine) by a pitcher who won at least 25 games. The only 20-game winner who went the distance fewer times than Welch was Bill Swift, who was 21-8 with just one complete game for the 1993 San Francisco Giants.

Lou Fette was 20-10 with a 2.88 ERA for the Boston Braves as a rookie in 1937 but won just 41 games in his career, 14 of which were shutouts. After his first season, Fette slipped to 11-13 in 1938 and then to 10-10 in 1939. He ended his career with a 0-5 mark in 1940 and a 0-2 record in 1945.

Paul Foytack is the only pitcher to give up home runs to four consecutive batters. The Angels' hurler surrendered homers to Woodie Held, Pedro Ramos, Tito Francona, and Larry Brown in the sixth inning of the second game of a doubleheader at Municipal Stadium on July 31, 1963, as the Angels lost 9-5 to Cleveland. Brown's home run against Foytack was his first in the major leagues.

The Cleveland Indians got just two hits during an April 12, 1992, doubleheader at Municipal Stadium against the Boston Red Sox – *yet managed to avoid getting swept.* In the opener, Boston's Matt Young pitched an eight-inning complete game and held the Tribe hitless, but he allowed seven walks and six stolen bases and lost 2-1. Due to a recent rule change that declared that no-hitters must go at least nine innings, Young did not even get credit for throwing a no-hitter. The new rule also deprived Boston's rookie catcher John Flaherty of the distinction of catching a no-hitter in his major league debut. Roger Clemens took the mound for the Red Sox in the second game and gave up just two hits – a single in the first to Carlos Baerga and a single in the third to Glenallen Hill – and struck out 12 while going the distance in 3-0 win.

Lefty Grove is the only pitcher to win 30 games in a season and have more wins than games started. Grove started in 30 games and worked in relief in 11 others for the 1931 Philadelphia A's, compiling a record of 31-4 with a 2.06 ERA.

On August 29, 2000, there were three one-hit games thrown in the major leagues. Boston's Pedro Martinez held the Devil Rays hitless until John Flaherty led off the bottom of the ninth with a single. Kris Benson and Josias Manzanillo of the Pirates combined to one-hit the Giants at Three Rivers Stadium, giving up just a first-inning single to Barry Bonds. Chan Ho Park and Mike Fetters led the Dodgers to a win over the Brewers at County Stadium, the only Milwaukee hit being a two-run homer by James Mouton off Park in the sixth.

On August 6, 2001, Boston's Scott Hatteberg pulled off a baseball first – *he hit into a triple play and smacked a grand slam in back-to-back at-bats.* In the fourth inning, with baserunners Brian Daubach and Chris Stynes moving on a 3-2 count, Hatteberg smashed a line drive to Rangers' shortstop Alex Rodriguez who flipped the ball to second base where Randy Velarde doubled off Daubach and tagged Stynes coming from first. Two innings later, Hatteberg arrived at the plate with the bases loaded and the Sox trailing 7-6 and crushed Juan Moreno's pitch deep into the Red Sox bullpen. The Sox held on to win 10-7 with rookie Casey Fossum getting first big league win.

In beating the Cubs 13-12 on April 21, 1991, the Pirates twice rallied from five runs down – *after the seventh inning.* Trailing 7-2 in the bottom of the eighth, the Bucs put four on the board thanks to a two-run triple by Orlando Merced and a two-run Bobby Bonilla homer. Gary Varsho's two-out double in the ninth plated Jeff King and knotted the score at 7-7. In the top of the 11th, the Cubs appeared to put the game away by scoring five runs, highlighted by Andre Dawson's grand slam. Pittsburgh had other ideas and scored two on a Jay Bell double plus single runs on Andy Van Slyke's sacrifice fly and Barry Bonds' single to make the score 12-11. Following a Gary

Redus walk to load the bases, Don Slaught completed the amazing comeback with a double to center that scored Bonilla and Bonds.

Only seven pitchers have won at least nine games in a season without suffering a loss. The first to do it was Joe Pate who was 9-0 in 47 games as a 34-year-old rookie for the 1926 Philadelphia A's – *and those nine games would be the only wins he would get.* He finished 0-3 in 32 games the following year and was out of the majors.

Philadelphia's Bill Kerksieck surrendered just 13 homers in his one big league season of 1939, but he still holds a share of two records – *because he gave up six of them in one game and four in one inning.* In a preview of things to come, Kerksieck gave up a homer to the very first batter he faced in the majors when Curt Davis of St. Louis took him deep in the seventh inning on June 21 at Sportsman's Park. On August 13, the New York Giants hammered Kerksieck and the Phillies 11-2 in the first of two games at the Polo Grounds. He gave up just seven hits in four innings – but six left the park. Frank Demaree connected against him in the first and third innings and then the Giants really pounded Kerksieck in the fourth with Alex Kampouris, Bill Lohrman, and Jo-Jo Moore hitting consecutive homers followed later by a blast from Zeke Bonura.

Randy Myers had eight seasons of at least 26 saves – *spread out among six different clubs.* He did it for the Mets (1988), Reds (1990), Padres (1992), Cubs (1993 and 1995), Orioles (1996 and 1997) and Blue Jays (1998).

Mike Hampton set the Houston Astro record for most wins in a season in his last game with the club and in the last regular season game in the Astrodome. Hampton upped his record to 22-4 as he pitched seven innings of three-hit ball, striking out eight, and led Houston to 9-4 win over Los Angeles on October 3, 1999. The win clinched the NL Central title for the Astros, and it moved Hampton past Joe Niekro, who won 21 for Houston in 1979, and edged him ahead of his teammate Jose Lima, who was 21-10 in 1999.

Four of the 15 perfect games in the major leagues since 1900 were decided by a 1-0 score – *and in each instance the losing pitcher pitched a complete game and the lone run was unearned.* On October 2, 1908, at Cleveland's League Park, Addie Joss matched up against Ed Walsh of Chicago and retired every White Sox hitter he faced. The only run scored in the third inning when Joe Birmingham led off with a single. Walsh caught Birmingham leaning toward second and picked him off, but Birmingham made it to third when Frank Isbell's throw to second base glanced off his shoulder and he eventually scored on a passed ball by catcher Ossee Schreckengost. Sandy Koufax and Bob Hendley hooked up in one of the greatest pitching duels of all time on September 9, 1965. Hendley allowed just one walk and one hit, a double to Lou Johnson in the seventh that landed just over first base and then rolled into foul territory, but Koufax was magnificent and struck out 14 Cubs. The Dodgers scored their only run in the fifth when Johnson walked. He was sacrificed to second by Ron Fairly, and then he stole third and scored when catcher Chris Krug's throw went into left field. On September 30, 1984, the final day of the season, the Angels' Mike Witt outdueled Charlie Hough of the Rangers with the Angels getting their only run in the sixth. Doug DeCinces singled, advanced to second when catcher Donnie Scott couldn't handle a knuckleball from Hough, and went to third on Brian Downing's ground ball. With the infield in, Reggie Jackson hit a grounder to first baseman Pete O'Brien who threw to the plate, but DeCinces beat the throw and scored – his run being unearned because of the passed ball. The next perfect game in the majors was by Tom Browning on September 16, 1988, at Cincinnati. Following a rain delay of 2 hours and 27 minutes, Browning took the mound against Tim Belcher and the Dodgers. The Reds pushed their lone run across the plate in the sixth. With two outs, Barry Larkin doubled, moved to third when Chris Sabo singled to third baseman Jeff Hamilton, and scored when Hamilton's throw bounced in the dirt and got away from first baseman Mickey Hatcher.

Through the 2005 season, Houston's Roy Oswalt is a perfect 15-0 in 19 games against the Cincinnati Reds – the most wins without a loss by a pitcher against one team. Oswalt beat them for his first career win by throwing 3.2 innings of relief at the Astrodome on May 14, 2001. Beginning on August 30, 2001, after he gave up a solo homer to Adam Dunn, he pitched 23 straight scoreless innings against the Reds before Barry Larkin singled in Juan Encarnacion on July 3, 2002. The closest that Oswalt has came to losing to Cincinnati was on August 1, 2004, when he trailed 5-3 after seven, but his teammates rallied for three in the eighth and another in the ninth to get him the win. In his first 19 appearances against the Reds, Oswalt has a 2.82 ERA with 104 strikeouts in 124.2 innings.

Randy Johnson had four games in which he struck out 18 or more batters – *but his record in those games was just 1-1.* Matched up against Nolan Ryan at Arlington Stadium on September 27, 1992, Johnson fanned 18 in only eight innings but got a no-decision as the Mariners lost 3-2. Ryan struck out five in seven innings and also did not figure in the decision. On June 24, 1997, Johnson set the American League record for strikeouts by a lefthanded pitcher by fanning 19 Oakland A's, yet he lost the game by a 4-1 score, thanks to Mark McGwire. McGwire had an RBI double in the third and then connected for a mammoth solo homer into the second deck of the Kingdome in the fifth inning. On August 8, 1997, Johnson matched his 19-strikeout performance and beat the Chicago White Sox 5-0 at the Kingdome. On May 8, 2001, against Cincinnati, Johnson (now with Arizona) recorded just the fourth instance of a pitcher striking out 20 batters in nine innings but left with the game tied 1-1 and got another no-decision.

Runs Batted In

Rickey Henderson is the only player to knock in over 1,000 runs without having a 75-RBI season. Henderson finished his career in 2003 season with 1,115 RBIs and a single-season high of 74 with New York Yankees in 1986. Ron Fairly is the only other player with more than 1,000 career RBIs who never topped 80 RBIs in any season. He drove in 1,044 runs with a career-best 77 RBIs for the 1963 Los Angeles Dodgers.

The only players since 1950 to drive in 100 runs while hitting fewer than ten home runs are Tommy Herr and Paul Molitor. Herr drove in 110 runs with only eight home runs for the 1985 St. Louis Cardinals. Molitor drove in 113 runs with just nine homers in 1996 for the Minnesota Twins.

Four players have driven in 100 runs while batting 400 or fewer times. Detroit's Rudy York was the first player to accomplish the feat he when drove in 103 runs in only 375 at-bats in 1937. The premature ending to the 1994 season due to the player's strike caused Frank Thomas and Jeff Bagwell to become the second and third players to do it, Thomas finishing with 101 RBIs in 399 at-bats while Bagwell ended with 116 RBIs in 400 at-bats. Barry Bonds drove in 101 runs in 2004 while walking a record 232 times and getting just 373 official at-bats.

On September 2, 1996, Mike Greenwell drove in all nine Boston runs in the Red Sox 9-8 victory over the Seattle Mariners. Greenwell had four of the seven Red Sox hits as he set the record for most RBIs in a game by a player who drove in all of his team's runs. Batting in the eighth spot, Greenwell hit a two-run homer in the fifth off Bob Wolcott to bring the Red Sox within 5-2 and a grand slam in the seventh off Bobby Ayala to put Boston in front 7-6. The Mariners rallied to retake the lead 8-6 only to watch Greenwell tie the game with an opposite-field double in the eighth against Norm Charlton. In the 10th inning with two on and two outs, Greenwell singled in the decisive run off Rafael Carmona.

The San Francisco Giants had a different player lead the National League in RBIs for three consecutive years. Will Clark topped the league with 109 RBIs in 1988, Kevin Mitchell led in 1989 with 125 RBIs, and Matt Williams knocked in 122 to pace the league in 1990.

Danny Tartabull had five 100-RBI seasons in his career – but his career high for RBIs was *just 102*. Tartabull had RBI totals of 101, 102, and 100 for the Kansas City Royals from 1987 to 1989 and later had 102 for the 1993 New York Yankees and 101 for the 1996 Chicago White Sox. A free agent following the 1996 season, Tartabull signed with the Phillies but broke his foot and appeared in just three games, going hitless in seven at-bats, before retiring at the end of the 1997 season. Those three games prevented him from becoming the first player to end his career following a 100-RBI season.

Bill Nicholson had only two 100-RBI seasons, yet each time it was good enough to lead the National League. He knocked in 128 runs in 1943 and 122 more in 1944 for the Chicago Cubs.

In 1993 Phil Plantier broke the record for fewest hits in a 100-RBI season when he drove in 100 runs while collecting just 111 hits for the San Diego Padres. The previous record was 115 hits by Rudy York of the 1937 Detroit Tigers. York collected his 103 RBIs by hitting .307 in only 375 at-bats. Plantier needed 462 at-bats to produce his 100 RBIs because he batted just .240.

Al Rosen had five consecutive 100-RBI seasons with the Cleveland Indians 1950 to 1954 – *but finished his career with only 717*

RBIs. Rosen topped the AL in RBIs in 1952 with 105 and again in 1953 when he knocked in 145, but the next two seasons his RBI totals slipped to 81 and 61 as nagging injuries began to take their toll on his play. Rosen retired following the 1956 season at the age of 32.

The 1965 Chicago Cubs had three players with more than 100 RBIs, but nobody else on the team drove in more than 34 runs. Billy Williams led the club with 108, followed by Ernie Banks who drove in 106 and Ron Santo who knocked in 101. Don Landrum was next with 34 and Glenn Beckert chipped in 30.

Tony Armas is the only player to drive in 100 or more runs in a season while batting less than .230. In 1983 with the Boston Red Sox, Armas collected only 125 hits in 574 at-bats for a batting average of .218, but he smacked 36 homers and drove in 107 runs.

Mike Piazza is the only player to drive in 100 or more runs in a season *while playing with three teams.* In 1998 Piazza started with the Los Angeles Dodgers and drove in 30 runs in 37 games before he was traded to Florida. With the Marlins, Piazza appeared in just five games and drove in five runs before being traded to the New York Mets where he collected 76 RBIs (in 109 games) to give him a total of 111 for the season.

Cincinnati's George Foster led the National League in RBIs for three consecutive years – *but never drove in 100 runs in any other season.* Foster knocked in 121 runs in 1976 to shatter his career high of 78 (set just one year earlier) and followed up with 149 RBIs in 1977 and 120 more in 1978. Limited by injuries to just 121 games in 1979, Foster slipped to 98 RBIs and then to 93 in 144 games in 1980. In 1981 Foster was on pace to drive in well over 100 runs, but the player's strike limited him to 90 RBIs in 108 games, and he finished one behind league-leader Mike Schmidt.

Mark Grudzielanek is the only player to hit at least 50 doubles in a season and produce fewer RBIs than doubles. Grudzielanek smacked 54 doubles in 1997 for the Montreal Expos but drove in just 51 runs. Pete Rose (51 doubles, 52 RBIs in 1978), Wade Boggs (51 doubles, 54 RBIs in 1989), and Brian Roberts (50 doubles, 53

RBIs in 2004) are the only other players to hit 50 doubles and drive in fewer than 70 runs.

The 1979 California Angels won the American League West behind the slugging of Don Baylor, Dan Ford and Bobby Grich. Baylor led the AL with 139 RBIs, while Ford and Grich each drove in 101 runs. It was the only time each of the three would top the 100-RBI mark in a season.

Smead Jolley had two 100-RBI seasons, yet only had 313 RBIs in his career. Jolley drove in 114 runs for the 1930 Chicago White Sox and 106 more in 1932 while splitting time between the White Sox and the Red Sox. Despite impressive offensive numbers for many seasons in the Pacific Coast League, his poor defense and lack of speed limited Jolley to just 473 major league games.

Lou Gehrig and Jimmie Foxx share the record of 13 consecutive 100-RBI seasons, ten of which overlapped. Beginning in 1926, Gehrig knocked in at least 112 runs per season for the New York Yankees until 1938, his last full season before his premature retirement in 1939. He led the American League in 1927, 1928, 1930, 1931 and 1934, knocking in over 150 runs seven times – including an American League record 184 RBIs in 1931. Foxx's streak was from 1929 to 1941, the first seven seasons with the Philadelphia A's and the last six with the Boston Red Sox. Foxx's low was 105 RBIs in both 1939 and 1941, and he surpassed 150 RBIs four times with a high of 175 in 1938. Foxx led the AL in 1932 and 1933 (with Gehrig as runner-up each year) and 1938.

After knocking in nine runs in just 24 games in 1932 and 1933 with the crosstown Cardinals, Ray Pepper moved over to the St. Louis Browns and drove in 101 runs in 148 games in 1934. The next season he slipped to 37 RBIs in 92 games and then drove in only 23 runs in his final season of 1936. Pepper ended his career with just 170 RBI – the fewest career RBIs by a player with a 100-RBI season.

Willie Mays drove in 1,903 runs in his career – *the eighth highest RBI total ever* – but never led the league in any one season. His closest finish to the National League leader was in 1964 when he drove in 111 runs and finished third in the National League, eight RBIs behind the St. Louis Cardinals' Ken Boyer.

Eddie Mathews and Mark McGwire are the only sluggers to hammer 500 homers and not drive in 1,500 runs. Mathews finished his career with 512 home runs and 1,453 RBIs while McGwire ended up with 583 home runs and drove in 1,414.

Jason Bay of the Pittsburgh Pirates had two eight-RBI games *before he collected his 50th career RBI.* After making his big league debut with San Diego on May 23, 2003, Bay was traded to the Pirates on August 26. Entering the first game of a September 19 doubleheader with six RBIs in 55 career at-bats, Bay knocked in the last eight of his season total of 14 RBIs. He hit a grand slam in the second, a two-run homer in the fourth and a two-run double in the fifth, all against Chicago's Carlos Zambrano. Despite Bay's big game, the Cubs won 10-9. Bay played in the second game and was hitless in four at-bats. On July 2, 2004, Bay duplicated his feat. After going 0-3 with a sacrifice fly in the first game of a twin bill against Milwaukee at PNC Park, he drove in eight in Pittsburgh's 13-2 romp in the second game. He had four hits (each against a different pitcher) including three, two-run doubles and a two-run homer. Bay's second eight-RBI game boosted his career total to 48 RBIs.

When Ozzie Smith hit .303 and drove in 75 runs for the 1987 St. Louis Cardinals, it made him the only player since 1940 to drive in 75 or more runs without hitting a home run.

The Baltimore Orioles began the 1998 season with the three active major league RBI leaders on their roster – Cal Ripken, Jr. (1,453 going into the 1998 season), Harold Baines (1,423), and Joe Carter (1,382).

Only five players have hit 35 home runs while driving in fewer than 85 runs – *and the first three did it in the same season.* Frank Robinson (38 homers, 83 RBIs), Willie Mays (36 and 84) and Wally Post (36 and 83) did it together in 1956. They were later joined by Barry Bonds (37 homers, 81 RBIs in the strike-shortened 1994 season) and Sammy Sosa (35 homers, 80 RBIs in 2004).

So Close

Don Buford never scored 100 runs in a season, but he is the only major league player to have three seasons of exactly 99 runs scored – *and he did it three years in a row.* In 1969 Buford scored his 99th run of the season when he homered to lead off the game against the Yankees on September 28, but then he failed to score in his final 17 plate appearances. His 99th run of 1970 also resulted from a homer, this time in the eighth inning against Washington on September 29, but again he did not to score another run, this time in his last 11 plate appearances. Buford entered the final game of the 1971 season with 97 runs and scored twice in his first three at-bats to get to 99 runs, but he fell just short again by not scoring in his final two trips to the plate.

Detroit Tiger great Al Kaline knocked out 146 hits in 1974, the most he had collected since 1964, to sneak past the 3,000-hit plateau and finish with a career hit total of 3,007. However, he retired just short of three other milestones – finishing his 22-year career with 399 home runs and 498 doubles and a .297 batting average.

Tommie Agee and Gene Alley are the only two players to finish with 999 hits – *and each got his last hit in the same park in the same year.* Agee, best known for his defensive excellence in the 1969 World Series with the New York Mets, finished his 12-year career with St. Louis in 1973. He got his last hit, a first-inning single against Steve Carlton, at Busch Stadium on September 29, 1973, but ended the season by going 0 for 3 in the rest of the game and 0 for 1 as a pinch hitter the next day. The Cardinals traded Agee to the Dodgers on December 5, but he was released in the spring of 1974 without making the Dodgers' club. Alley played shortstop from 1963 to 1973 for the Pirates, getting his final hit on July 4, 1973, at Busch Stadium when he singled to right in the fifth against Tom Murphy. Unlike Agee, who had only four chances for his 1,000th hit, Alley played in 24 more games but went 0 for 20 to end his career.

Dodgers' outfielder Carl Furillo finished his career with 1,910 hits in 6,378 at-bats, resulting in a career batting average of .29947 – just *one more hit* during his 15-year career would have rounded his career mark up to .300. After winning the NL batting title in 1953, Furillo's lifetime average stood at .301, and then hovered right at the .300 mark at the end of the each of the next six seasons, except for 1955 when it was .301. Furillo rounded down to .299 when he returned for the 1960 season, and collected just two hits in ten at-bats. Through 2005, he has the most hits of any player who ended his career with a .299 batting average.

Philadelphia Phillie Lefty O'Doul almost hit .400 in 1929 – despite not being able to hit against the pitching staff that allowed the *highest* batting average to opposing batters. O'Doul hit .398 yet did not have the luxury of batting against his own teammates. The 1929 Phillies' staff yielded a league-high .319 average, 17 points higher than the next worst pitching staff and 25 points higher than the National League average.

Tony Cuccinello lost the closest batting race in baseball history – and then *never* appeared in another major league game. The 37-year-old third baseman collected 124 hits in 402 at-bats in 1945 for the Chicago White Sox yet was cut by the team in January 1946 when many of the game's younger players returned from serving in World War II. The Yankees' Snuffy Stirnweiss got three hits on the final day to finish the season 195 for 632 and edge Cuccinello by .000087 (.3085443 to .3084577). Cuccinello was denied a chance to catch Stirnweiss when Chicago's last game was rained out. His teammate, Johnny Dickshot, finished third in league batting race at .302 (the only other AL regular to hit .300) and his career also ended with the 1945 season.

At the age of 45, Carlton Fisk began the 1993 season for the Chicago White Sox with a bang by hitting a solo homer in his first at-bat on April 7 against Minnesota's Jim Deshaies. Fisk appeared in 25 more games and batted 50 more times, getting just nine more hits, all singles, and was released on June 28 shortly after breaking Bob Boone's record for most games played as a catcher. He finished his career with 3,999 total bases – *just one base shy of becoming the only catcher to reach 4,000 total bases.*

During his MVP season of 1984, Ryne Sandberg missed by one triple and one home run of becoming the only player to get at least 200 hits, 20 doubles, 20 triples, 20 home runs and 20 steals in one season. Sandberg's last homer in 1984 was on September 12 at Wrigley Field against Montreal's Rick Grapenthin. After collecting his National League-leading 19th triple on September 20 against Pittsburgh's Don Robinson, Sandberg batted 33 more times without a triple or homer. Sandberg would later have six seasons of at least 20 homers, but would never hit more than eight triples in any other season.

Making his 400th career start on July 29, 1999, Mike Morgan came within inches of giving up Cal Ripken's 400th home run. Ripken rifled a ball to left field in the third inning that hit just below the home run line on the left field wall at Camden Yards and was ruled in play, resulting in a double for the Baltimore shortstop. If Ripken's hit had made it out of the park, Morgan would have had the distinction of serving up the 400th home run of two Hall of Famers because as a 19-year-old rookie with the Oakland A's he surrendered Carl Yastrzemski's 400th home run on July 24, 1979, at Fenway Park. Morgan limited the Orioles to just three hits and one earned run in six innings, beating them for the time since September 6, 1985.

In 2001 Greg Maddux set the National League record by pitching 72.1 innings without a walk. His streak ending on August 12 when he *intentionally* walked both Steve Finley and Damian Miller in the third inning of a loss to Arizona. Maddux's next unintentional pass did not happen until August 22 when he walked San Diego's Ben Davis. If not for the two intentional walks against Arizona, Maddux would have pitched 84.2 innings without a free pass, breaking Bill Fischer's 1962 record of 84.1 innings consecutive innings without a walk.

On September 2, 2001, Mike Mussina retired the first 26 Red Sox before Carl Everett lined a two-strike pitch to left-center for a single to end his bid for a perfect game, but Mussina retired the next hitter to win the game 1-0. The losing pitcher was David Cone, who had pitched a perfect game on July 18, 1999, against Montreal. If not for Everett's hit, Cone would have become the only pitcher to both win *and* lose a perfect game.

On October 3, 1937, Cleveland's Johnny Allen entered the last game of the season with a record of 15-0, needing a win to equal the American League record of 16 consecutive victories. Allen pitched a complete game, giving up just five hits and one run on an RBI single by Hank Greenberg in the first inning, but Detroit's Jake Wade was even better – allowing just a single to Hal Trosky. Wade's shutout was his only one in 25 starts in 1937 and was the second of his three career shutouts. The 1-0 loss also kept Allen from setting the record for most wins in a season without suffering a loss, a record that still belongs to Tom Zachary who was 12-0 for the Yankees in 1929.

The Cincinnati Reds set the National League record by putting together a streak of 208 consecutive games without getting shut out. The Reds began their streak with the first game of the 2000 season and it finally ended on May 24, 2001, when Chicago's Jon Lieber pitched a one-hitter and blanked them 3-0 at Wrigley Field. Cincinnati's streak fell short of the record 308-game streak set by the 1931-33 Yankees but would have easily surpassed the Yankees' streak if not for the Reds' participation in a one-game playoff for the 1999 National League wild card. The Reds finished the 1999 season at 96-66, tied with the New York Mets for the wild card spot. In the playoff game they were beaten 5-0 by Al Leiter who yielded just two hits and struck out seven while recording his *only* shutout of the year. Prior to being shut out by Leiter, the last game in which the Reds failed to score was against the Braves back on April 30, 1999. So if not for the extra regular season game against New York to determine the NL Wild Card team, Cincinnati would have scored in 349 consecutive regular season games and broken the Yankees' record.

Lonnie Smith almost became the only player win a World Series with four different teams. Smith played on the winning team in the Series in 1980 with the Phillies, in 1982 with the Cardinals and in 1985 with the Royals. Looking for his fourth World Series win, he returned to the Series with the 1991 and 1992 Braves but lost each time. The Braves lost the 1991 Series by dropping both the sixth and seventh games in extra innings, with Smith playing a crucial role in the Game 7 loss. With the game scoreless in the eighth, he lost sight of the ball on Terry Pendleton's double and instead of scoring easily was forced to stop at third base. The Braves eventually lost 1-0 in ten innings.

The 1979 Milwaukee Brewers made it until the last day of the season without getting shutout – but were then blanked 5-0 by Jerry Koosman and the Minnesota Twins. The Brewers started the September 30 game against the Twins with consecutive singles by Jim Gantner and Robin Yount, but the rally was squelched when Gantner was thrown out attempting to advance to third on Dick Davis' fly out to right. Gorman Thomas led off the fourth with a double and was left stranded, as was Lenn Sakata when he got to second with one out in the fifth. Milwaukee's last good scoring chance was in the ninth. Following a Don Money ground out, Ray Fosse collected his last big league hit by tripling to left field, but the rally was killed when Jim Wohlford followed with a grounder to third baseman John Castino who tagged out Fosse when he wandered too far from the third base bag. The loss prevented the Brewers from joining the 1932 Yankees and the 2000 Reds as the only teams to go an entire season without getting shut out.

In 1949 Ted Williams missed out on an unprecedented third Triple Crown because he lost the second-closest batting race in major league history. Williams led the league with 43 home runs and 159 RBIs, but Detroit's George Kell edged out Williams by .00015 to take the batting crown. Kell went 2 for 3 on the last day of the season to finish with 179 hits in 522 at-bats for an average of .34291. Williams was hitless in two at-bats on the final day and ended at .34276 (194 hits in 566 at-bats).

Sam Crawford finished second in the batting race four times without ever winning one. Crawford was with Cincinnati in 1902 when he finished runner-up in the National League race to Pittsburgh's Ginger Beaumont, .357 to .333. The next year Crawford began a 15-year career with Detroit in the American League by batting .335, second to Nap Lajoie's .344. In both 1907 and 1908, Crawford was beaten by his Tiger teammate Ty Cobb, hitting .323 to Cobb's .350 in 1907 and .311 to Cobb's .324 in 1908.

New York Yankees' great Whitey Ford finished with a career record of 236-106. In his last two seasons of 1966 and 1967, Ford had a combined record of 4-9, which lowered his career winning percentage from .705 to .690 and kept him from being the only pitcher with 200 wins and a winning percentage greater than .700.

Cleveland's Dick Bosman pitched a 4-0 no-hitter against the defending World Series champion Oakland A's on July 19, 1974, but missed hurling a perfect game *due to his own throwing error.* With two outs in the fourth, Bosman fielded Sal Bando's slow hopper to the right side of the mound and made an off-balance throw which glanced off first baseman Tom McCraw's glove, allowing Bando to reach first safely and advance to second.

Joey Jay ended his pitching career in 1966 with 99 wins and 999 strikeouts. Traded from the Reds to the Braves on June 15, 1966, Jay started eight games for Atlanta and was 0-4. His last career appearance was in relief against his former team during a 4-2 Atlanta win on October 2. Jay entered in the bottom of the seventh, just *after* the Braves pushed a run across to break a scoreless tie for starter Ron

Reed. Jay pitched three innings and contributed a two-run double in the bottom of the eighth before giving up two runs in the bottom of the ninth. Because Jay entered the game after Atlanta took a lead that they never lost, Reed received the victory and Jay stayed at 99 career wins. Jay also failed to record a single strikeout in his three innings of work and remained stuck on 999.

The 2003 Detroit Tigers lost 119 games, just missing the 1962 Mets' modern record of 120 losses. An 11th-inning homer from Minnesota's Michael Cuddyer beat the Tigers 5-4 on September 26, handing them their 119th loss with just two more games to play. The next day Detroit seemed destined to tie the Mets' record of futility when they trailed 8-0 in the fifth inning. However, they rallied with a run in the fifth, plated three more in the seventh and, thanks to four walks by the Minnesota pitchers, tied it with four runs in the eighth. They completed their comeback by winning the game 9-8 in the bottom of the ninth against Jesse Orosco when Alex Sanchez walked with one out, stole two bases, and scored on a wild pitch. The comeback was Detroit's biggest since June 20, 1965, and gave Jesse Orosco the last loss of his 24-year career. In the season's final game with the game tied 2-2, the Tigers exploded for seven runs in the sixth inning – *their biggest inning of the year* – to win 9-4.

Randy Johnson, one of just three pitchers with 4,000 strikeouts, just missed joining Nolan Ryan with 2,000 in each league. Johnson left the Diamondbacks after the 2004 season with 1,999 strikeouts in the National League and joined the AL's New York Yankees. Entering the 2006 season, the big lefthander has fanned 2,373 batters in the American League.

Cleveland's Al Rosen led the American League in 1953 with 43 home runs and 145 RBIs – and missed winning the Triple Crown when he narrowly failed to beat out a grounder in his last at-bat of the season. Rosen entered the final day of the season trailing Washington's Mickey Vernon for the batting title, .336 to .333. Rosen hit safely three times in his first four at-bats against the Tigers, but Vernon was 2 for 3 against the A's by that time and still had a slight lead. Needing a base hit in his 599th at-bat to take the crown, Rosen hit a tough grounder to third and almost beat the throw to first. Following Rosen's ground out, Vernon batted one more time in Washington and lined out to right to win the title .33717 to .33556. If Rosen had gotten a hit in his final at-bat, he would have edged Vernon by .000058.

On August 31, 1968, Pittsburgh's Roy Face tied Walter Johnson's record for most pitching appearances (802) with one team – and was then sold by the club *before* he had a chance to break it. Steve Blass started for the Pirates and got the first out before moving to left field as Face entered the game and retired the next batter, Felix Millan. Face then left the game, and Blass took back over on the mound. Blass finished the game, allowing just five hits and winning 8-0, but he did not get credit for a shutout because Face had retired a hitter. Following the game, the Pirates announced the sale of Face to the Detroit Tigers.

Minnesota played their first game in the Metrodome on April 6, 1982, and Gary Gaetti just missed becoming the first player to hit three homers on opening day and the first player to hit three homers in the first game of a new ballpark. The Twins' rookie tripled to center in the second inning off Seattle's Floyd Bannister but was thrown out at the plate attempting to stretch his three-bagger into an inside-the-park homer. In his next two at-bats against Bannister, Gaetti hit homers in the fourth and seventh, and later he added an RBI single in the eighth against reliever Mike Stanton, but the Mariners prevailed 11-7.

Entering the final game of the 2004 season, 46-year-old Julio Franco had 97 hits and was trying to become the oldest player to get 100 hits in a season. Franco singled in each of his first two at-bats and walked in the sixth against Chicago's Greg Maddux before he struck out looking in the eighth against Jon Leicester to end the year with 99 hits.

Ken Phelps of the Oakland A's ended Seattle's Brian Holman's bid for a perfect game on April 20, 1990, with two-out home run in the ninth inning – *his only home run of the season and the last of his career.* With the A's trailing 6-0, Phelps pinch-hit and smashed Holman's first pitch deep over the right field wall at Oakland-Alameda County Coliseum. Holman recovered to strikeout Rickey Henderson to finish with a one-hitter.

In the eight-team major leagues, prior to expansion and the 162-game schedule, no team swept all 22 games against another club, but four clubs did post 21-1 marks against a league opponent, with two of them came particularly close to sweeping. The fabled 1927 New York Yankees won their first 21 games against the hapless St. Louis Browns. In their last meeting on September 11 at Yankee Stadium, the Browns started fast by scoring one in the first and then broke a 1-1 tie with four runs in the fourth inning, highlighted by a two-run triple from George Sisler. Although Babe Ruth hit his 50th homer in the bottom of the frame, the Browns held on for a 6-2 win. The Chicago Cubs were 21-1 against the Cincinnati Reds in 1945, including seven doubleheader sweeps, with their lone loss coming by a single run. After losing the first 15 meetings, the Reds finally broke through with a 4-3 win on August 4 at Crosley Field. Trailing 3-1 in the fifth, they rallied for two runs to tie the game and then took the lead on a single by starting pitcher Ed Heusser. The Cubs threatened in the top of the ninth, but Lennie Merullo was thrown out on a close play at third attempting to stretch his leadoff double into a triple, resulting in the ejection of manger Charlie Grimm who protested the call.

Dave Stieb pitched three games in which he lost a no-hitter *with two men out in the ninth inning.* On September 24, 1988, at Cleveland, Stieb appeared to have held the Indians hitless, but Julio Franco's routine grounder with two outs hit the seam where the turf met the infield dirt and took a bad hop over the second baseman's head for a single. In his very next start on September 30 at Toronto, Stieb was again one out from a "no-no" when Baltimore's Jim Traber singled to break it up. Stieb retired the first 26 Yankees he faced on August 4, 1989, but lost his bid for a perfect game when Roberto Kelly doubled to left. Stieb eventually got a no-hitter when he beat the Indians 3-0 at Cleveland on September 2, 1990.

Teams

In the first 102 seasons of their storied rivalry, Boston's largest margin of victory against the New York Yankees was a 15-1 win on September 1, 1990, at Fenway Park – *then they beat New York by 16 runs twice in less than two months.* On May 28, 2005, the Red Sox pounded four New York pitchers at Yankee Stadium for a 17-1 victory. The onslaught was led by Johnny Damon (4 hits, 3 runs), Manny Ramirez (4 hits, RBI), Edgar Renteria (3 hits, 5 RBIs), and Trot Nixon (3 hits, 5 RBIs). Back in Boston on July 15, David Ortiz had a homer and drove in five runs to go with Trot Nixon's inside-the-park homer and five RBIs as the Sox duplicated the 17-1 score.

The Braves never had losing season while in Milwaukee from 1953 to 1965. Their season win totals varied from a high of 95 in 1957 when they won the World Series to a low of 83 in 1961. Meanwhile, the A's never had a winning season during their stay in Kansas City from 1955 to 1967. They lost over 100 games four times as their victories totals ranged from a low of 52 in 1956 to a high of 74 in 1966.

Through the 1994 season, the Los Angeles Dodgers' 1977 club was the only team to have four 30-homer players, but then the Colorado Rockies moved into Coors Field in 1995 and did it *four times in the next five seasons* (1995-1997 and 1999). Three of the four players on the 1996 and 1997 Colorado squads also topped the 40-homer mark – a feat previously achieved only by the 1973 Atlanta Braves.

Casey Stengel wore the uniform of four different New York teams. Stengel played for Brooklyn Dodgers from 1912 to 1917 and the Giants from 1921 to 1923. Following his playing days, he managed the Dodgers from 1934 to 1936, the Yankees from 1949 to 1960, and the Mets from 1962 to 1965.

The 1938 Chicago Cubs won the National League pennant by two games over the Pittsburgh Pirates, *yet no player on the team drove in 70 runs.* Seven Cubs' players did drive in at least 56 runs, led by Augie Galan's team high 69 RBIs. Much of the credit for Chicago's pennant belongs to their pitching staff, which led the National League in 1938 with a 3.37 earned run average and 16 shutouts, and their defense, which committed a NL-low 135 errors.

Only two pitching staffs have produced four 20-game winners in a season. The 1920 Chicago White Sox won 96 games and finished second in the AL, two games behind Cleveland. Their staff consisted of Red Faber (23-13), Lefty Williams (22-14), Dickie Kerr (21-9), and Eddie Cicotte (21-10). The foursome accounted for 87 of the 96 White Sox wins, with Roy Wilkinson (7-9), George Payne (1-1), and Shovel Hodge (1-1) winning the other nine. The 1971 Baltimore Orioles won the American League East with 101 wins. Dave McNally led the O's with a record of 21-5, followed by Pat Dobson (20-8), Mike Cuellar (20-9), and Jim Palmer (20-9). Dick Hall was next on the staff with six wins, appearing in 27 games out of the bullpen and going 6-6.

The 1929 Philadelphia Phillies and the 1937 Detroit Tigers are the only two teams to have four players collect at least 200 hits. The Phillies were led by Lefty O'Doul who collected a National League record 254 hits. Chuck Klein followed with 219, Fresco Thompson added 202, and Pinky Whitney had an even 200. Gee Walker topped the Tigers in 1937 with 213 hits, Charlie Gehringer collected 209, Pete Fox had 208, and Hank Greenberg finished with exactly 200.

From 1991 to 1998, an Atlanta Brave pitcher either led or tied for the National League lead in wins each season. Tom Glavine tied for the league lead with 20 wins in both 1991 and 1992 and with 22 victories in 1993. Greg Maddux tied for the NL lead in 1994 with 16 wins and followed that with a league-high 19 wins in 1995. John Smoltz led in 1996 by winning 24 games, followed by Denny Neagle who led with 20 wins in 1997, and then by Tom Glavine who led again in 1998 with 20 wins. Houston's Mike Hampton broke the Braves' string in 1999 when he won 22 games, but Glavine came back in 2000 to top the NL again with 21 victories.

The Dodgers moved from Brooklyn to Los Angeles for the 1958 season, and it took 46 years to produce a National League home run champion. Their drought ended in 2004 when Adrian Beltre topped the league with 48 homers. The Giants moved from New York the same year and have had 11 home run champions since they arrived in San Francisco – Orlando Cepeda (1961), Willie Mays (1962, 1964, and 1965), Willie McCovey (1963, 1968, and 1969), Kevin Mitchell (1989), Barry Bonds (1993 and 2001), and Matt Williams (1994). However, since the move to the West Coast, the Dodgers have won nine NL pennants and five World Series while the Giants have appeared in just three World Series and lost all three.

After the 1993 season, *their first year of existence*, the Colorado Rockies boasted a National League batting champion – a feat that neither the New York Mets nor the Houston Astros have achieved since they joined the NL in 1962. Andres Galarraga led all National League batters with a .370 average during the Rockies' inaugural season. The Rockies moved into Coors Field for the 1995 season and began a streak in which they led the National League in team batting average for the next eight seasons. The streak ended in 2003 when they finished fourth in the NL with a .267 average. During their streak they produced four more batting champions – Larry Walker (.363 in 1998, .379 in 1999, and .350 in 2001) and Todd Helton (.372 in 2000).

The 1990 Kansas City Royals had both reigning Cy Young Award winners on their pitching staff. In 1989 KC's Bret Saberhagen compiled a record of 23-6 with a 2.16 earned run average to win the American League Cy Young while San Diego's Mark Davis was 4-3 with a league-leading 44 saves and captured the award in the National League. In the off-season, the free-agent Davis joined Saberhagen by signing with the Royals, but neither pitcher could duplicate his previous year's numbers in the 1990 season – Saberhagen went 5-9 with a 3.27 ERA and Davis was 2-7 with only six saves.

Rogers Hornsby holds the highest single-season batting average *for three different teams.* Hornsby batted a major league record .424 for the St. Louis Cardinals in 1924, hit .387 for the 1928 Boston Braves in his only year with the team, and followed that with an average of .380 for the Chicago Cubs in 1929. Hornsby also briefly held the New York Giants' record with his .361 average in 1927 (his only year with the Giants) until his mark was surpassed by Bill Terry's .372 in 1929. Over the five-year span from 1921 to 1925, Hornsby *averaged* over .400, posting season batting averages of .397, .401, .384, .424, and .403 while getting 1,078 hits in 2,679 at-bats for a batting average of .402.

As the New York Mets made their drive toward the 1969 National League Eastern Division Championship, they swept a doubleheader from the Pirates at Forbes Field on September 12, winning each game by a 1-0 score – *with the run in each game being driven in by the Mets' starting pitcher.* In the opener, Jerry Koosman pitched a complete game, giving up only three hits, and got his only RBI of the season when he drove in Bobby Pfeil with a single to right in the fifth inning off Pirates' pitcher Bob Moose. In the second game, Don Cardwell singled against Dock Ellis to score Bud Harrelson in the second and held the Pirates to only four hits in eight innings. The sweep pushed New York's winning streak to nine games and ran their streak of scoreless innings to 34 straight.

The St. Louis Cardinals finished last in the majors in home runs every year from 1982 to 1991 except for 1985 when they were next-to-last, just seven home runs ahead of the Pittsburgh Pirates. During this ten-year span, St. Louis averaged 74.9 homers per season, with a high of 94 in 1987 and a low of 58 in 1986. Although they did not hit with much power, the Cardinals used speed, good pitching and excellent defense to win three pennants (1982, 1985, and 1987) and the 1982 World Series. They won the 1987 NL pennant despite not having a single pitcher win 12 games – Greg Mathews, Danny Cox, and Bob Forsch each won 11, John Tudor chipped in ten, and Ken Dayley and Joe Magrane won nine each.

Three players with over 3,000 career hits played together for the 1928 Philadelphia Athletics. Ty Cobb and Tris Speaker finished their big league careers with the A's in 1928. Cobb got his final 114 hits in 353 at-bats while Speaker batted 191 times and got the last 51 hits of his career. Eddie Collins was 10 for 33, mostly as a pinch hitter, in 36 games with the A's in 1928 and would hang on to make brief appearances with them in the next two seasons, going hitless in seven at-bats in 1929 and collecting his last hit (in only two at-bats) in 1930. The Hall of Fame trio appeared in several games together but never collected hits in the same game.

The Seattle Mariners began play in the American League in 1977 and were blanked 7-0 and 2-0 by the California Angels in their first two games, finally scoring in the fourth inning in their third game when Dan Meyer doubled in Dave Collins. The Mariners went on to suffer 14 consecutive losing seasons before finally breaking the .500 mark in 1991 with a record of 83-79.

On May 9, 1984, the Chicago White Sox and Milwaukee Brewers completed the longest game in American League history. The game had begun the day before but was suspended after 17 innings with the score tied at 3-3. The Brewers had taken the lead by scoring twice in the top of the ninth, but the White Sox scored two in the bottom of the inning to force the game into extra innings. Neither team scored again until Milwaukee's Ben Oglivie hammered a three-run homer in the top of the 21st inning. However, the White Sox rallied to retie the game with an RBI single from Carlton Fisk and a two-run single by Tom Paciorek. Harold Baines finally ended the marathon when he hit a solo homer with one out against Chuck Porter, who pitched 7.1 innings in relief, in the bottom of the 25th. Tom Seaver got the win by pitching the 25th inning for the White Sox and then started the originally scheduled game for May 9, pitching 8.1 innings to pick up another win as Chicago beat Milwaukee 5-4.

On June 22, 1998, an interleague game allowed Dwight Gooden the opportunity to pitch the Cleveland Indians to a 3-1 win over the Chicago Cubs at Wrigley Field. It was Gooden's last career win against Chicago and raised his lifetime record against them to 28-4, including 11 complete games. Gooden also recorded the first of three career saves against Chicago at Wrigley Field on September 19, 1989. Making his second relief appearance after a stint on the disabled list, Gooden gave up three hits and one run in four innings as the Mets beat the Cubs 5-2.

Only two teams have produced two 30-30 players in the same season. The 1987 New York Mets had Darryl Strawberry (39 homers, 36 steals) and Howard Johnson (36 and 32). Ellis Burks (40 and 32) and Dante Bichette (31 and 31) did it for the Colorado Rockies in 1996. For Strawberry, Burks, and Bichette their 30-30 season was the only season they would reach 30 steals.

Of the seven teams to score 1,000 runs since 1900, the 1999 Cleveland Indians (1,009 runs) are the only one to do so since the 1950 Boston Red Sox, making them the only team to do it since the schedule expanded from 154 to 162 games in 1961. The 1996 Seattle Mariners came close by scoring 993 times in just 161 games. The record for runs scored is 1,067 by the 1931 New York Yankees.

The Atlanta Braves won the first 16 games and 29 of the first 33 games that they played against the Colorado Rockies. The Braves' 13-0 record against the expansion Rockies in 1993, including a three game sweep to end the season, helped them to a record of 104-58 and the National League West pennant over the San Francisco Giants. The Giants were 10-3 against the Rockies and finished the season at 103-59, one game behind the Braves.

Only five teams have posted three consecutive 100-win seasons – the Philadelphia A's (1929-1931), St. Louis Cardinals (1942-1944), Baltimore Orioles (1969-1971), Atlanta Braves (1997-1999) and New

York Yankees (2002-2004). The Braves and Yankees are the only ones of the group that did not to win at least one World Series during their three-year run.

Frank Chance stole 67 bases for the Chicago Cubs in 1903 – *and still holds the team record for thefts.* Bill Maloney (59 steals in 1905) and Chance (57 in 1906) also topped the 50-steal barrier for the Cubs early in the 20th century. Ryne Sandberg (54 in 1985) and Eric Young (54 in 2000) are the only Cubs' players since 1906 to steal more than 50 bases in a season.

During their stay in the Kingdome from 1977 to June 27, 1999, the Seattle Mariners never swept the Baltimore Orioles in any series of three or more games, although they did take two of three on 14 different occasions. Then they moved to Safeco Field and swept the O's three straight from July 30 to August 1, 1999, during Baltimore's *first visit* to the new park.

Mike Morgan holds the record for playing for the most different teams. From 1978 to 2002, Morgan appeared for 12 teams and compiled a career record of 141-186. He pitched for Oakland (2-13), the New York Yankees (7-11), Toronto (0-3), Seattle (24-35), Baltimore (1-6), Los Angeles (33-36), the Chicago Cubs (30-35), St. Louis (9-14), Cincinnati (11-15), Minnesota (4-2), Texas (13-10) and Arizona (7-6).

Journeyman Phil Roof played for three new teams in his career. After his second season with the Kansas City A's, Roof moved to Oakland with them and stayed with the club for two more seasons before being dealt on January 15, 1970, to the Milwaukee Brewers who were joining the AL for the upcoming season. Roof's last major league action was in 1977 when he batted five times in three games for the expansion Toronto Blue Jays.

Eddie Mathews is the only player to play for the Braves while they were in Boston, Milwaukee, and Atlanta. Mathews appeared in 145 games with the Braves in 1952, the last year they were in Boston, and was a regular during the 13 years that they were in Milwaukee.

Mathews played in 134 games in 1966, his last year with the Braves and their first year in Atlanta.

The 2003 Boston Red Sox are the only squad since 1900 to have eight players with 80 or more RBIs – Nomar Garciaparra (104), Manny Ramirez (104), David Ortiz (101), Kevin Millar (95), Trot Nixon (87), Todd Walker (85), Bill Mueller (85), and Jason Varitek (85).

The 1961 New York Yankees' record of 240 home runs in a season lasted until 1996 – *but was then broken by three teams in the same season.* In 1996 the Baltimore Orioles blasted 257 homers, the Seattle Mariners crushed 245, and the Oakland A's hammered 243. Baltimore's new record lasted only until the next season when the Mariners, led by 56 homers from Ken Griffey, Jr. and 40 more from Jay Buhner, blasted 264 home runs.

During the 1950s, the Cleveland Indians finished second to the New York Yankees in the American League five times in six years. The Tribe finished five games behind New York in 1951, two games back in 1952 and 8 1/2 games back in 1953. In 1954 the Indians finally broke through against the Yankees by winning 111 games, an American League record that would stand until the 1998 Yankees won 114. Unfortunately for Cleveland, they ran into another New York team, the Giants, in the 1954 World Series and were swept in four games. In 1955 the Indians dropped back to three games behind the Yankees and then finished nine games back in 1956.

The San Diego Padres have not had a player hit for the cycle since they joined the National League in 1969. The Philadelphia A's, on the other hand, once had three players hit for the cycle *in a span of just 12 days.* On August 3, 1933, A's catcher Mickey Cochrane pulled it off against the Yankees at New York, followed by a cycle from Pinky Higgins at Washington on August 6, and one by Jimmie Foxx at Cleveland on August 14.

The 1984 Pittsburgh Pirates led the National League in ERA – *and still finished last.* Anchored by Rick Rhoden (2.72 ERA in

238.1 innings), John Candelaria (2.72 ERA in 185.1 innings) and Larry McWilliams (2.93 ERA in 227.1 innings), the Pirates' staff had a 3.11 ERA and finished third in the NL with 995 strikeouts. The Pirates' poor season was due to their dismal hitting as they struggled to finish ninth in the league in homers and 10th in runs scored. Pittsburgh finished with a 75-87 record and in last place in the NL East – a full 21 1/2 games behind the Chicago Cubs – and ahead of only Cincinnati (70-92) and San Francisco (66-96) in the entire National League.

In 2001 the Seattle Mariners tied the 1906 Chicago Cubs' record of 116 regular season wins. The Mariners would have broken the record if they had not blown two 12-run leads against Cleveland on August 5. Seattle led 12-0 after two innings and 14-2 entering the seventh inning, only to see the Indians rally to tie the game by scoring three runs in the seventh, four more in the eighth and another five (all with two outs) in the ninth. Cleveland then completed their remarkable comeback by winning 15-14 on Jolbert Cabrera's single in the bottom of the 11th. The Indians' rally matched the biggest comeback in major league history, accomplished only two other times – by the Detroit Tigers against the Chicago White Sox on June 18, 1911, and by the Philadelphia Athletics against the Indians on June 15, 1925.

Through the 1999 season the Chicago White Sox had never hit 200 homers in a season but have now done it six years in a row.

Year	Team Leader	Team Total
2000	Frank Thomas (42)	216
2001	Paul Konerko (32)	214
2002	Magglio Ordonez (38)	217
2003	Frank Thomas (42)	220
2004	Paul Konerko (41)	242
2005	Paul Konerko (40)	200

The Minnesota Twins have not had a 30-homer player since 1987 when Kent Hrbek (34), Tom Brunansky (32), and Gary Gaetti (31) each topped the mark. From 1988 to 2005, players from the other major league teams combined for 464 seasons of at least 30 homers, but the best seasons by a Twins' player were 29-homer years by Chili Davis in 1991 and Torii Hunter in 2002.

On September 9, 2004, the Kansas City Royals set a team record for runs scored in a doubleheader – *despite getting shut out in the second game.* The Royals pounded the Detroit Tigers in the opening game 26-5, led by Joe Randa who became the first AL player to get six hits and score six runs in a game. In their 11-run third inning, Kansas City tied the AL record by having 13 consecutive hitters reach base – two doubles, three walks and eight singles. In the second game, Detroit's Jeremy Bonderman held the Royals to six hits in eight innings and cruised to an 8-0 win.

The Chicago White Sox were the last of the original 16 major league franchises to have a 30-homer player (Bill Melton, 1970), a 40-homer player (Frank Thomas, 1993) and have a player hit an All-Star game home run (Frank Thomas, 1995).

Following their 1997 World Series victory, the Florida Marlins traded away several key players and ended up just 54-108 in 1998. They were *winless* against three teams, going 0-9 against the Milwaukee Brewers, Cincinnati Reds, and San Francisco Giants.

The 1979 New York Mets lost four consecutive doubleheaders at Shea Stadium – *within a span of five days.* The streak started on September 18 when the Cubs beat them 2-0 and 2-1 in 11 innings. Montreal then came to town and took two games from New York on both September 19 and 20. After an off-day, the Mets dropped two to the Cardinals on September 22. During the doubleheader sweeps New York was outscored 28 to 11.

The Pittsburgh Pirates were the last of the original franchises to produce a Rookie of the Year winner. The ROY Award began in 1947, but 57 years passed before Jason Bay finally broke through for the Pirates in 2004 and claimed the trophy by hitting .282 with 28 homers with 82 RBIs. The Pirates are also the only one of the 16 original franchises without a 200-homer season. Their best year was 1999 when they smacked 171 home runs, led by Brian Giles who hit 39. Despite not having a hitter lead the league in hitting since 1983, the Pirates have produced more batting champions (24) than any other team – Honus Wagner (8), Roberto Clemente (4), Paul Waner (3), Dave Parker (2), Bill Madlock (2), Ginger Beaumont, Arky Vaughan, Debs Garms, Dick Groat and Matty Alou.

In the 1916 season, Joe Bush and Elmer Myers combined to win 29 games – *for a team that only won 36 games.* The 1916 Philadelphia A's were a miserable 36-117 and finished last, 40 games behind the seventh-place Senators. Bush compiled a record of 15-24 in 40 games and Myers was 14-23 in 44 games. Teammates Jack Nabors (1-20), Tom Sheehan (1-16), Jing Johnson (2-8) and rookie Socks Seibold (1-2) also picked up wins. The A's other two victories were by Rube Parnham who was 2-1 in four games, making him the only pitcher on the A's staff to have a winning record.

Only two teams in baseball history have produced four players with 30 homers and still hit less than 200 homers as a team – *both times by the Los Angels Dodgers.* In the 1977 season Steve Garvey (33), Reggie Smith (32), Dusty Baker (30) and Ron Cey (30) became the first four teammates to each hit 30 homers. Steve Yeager was next with 16 and Rick Monday added 15 more as the Dodgers hit 191 long balls. Twenty years later for the 1997 Dodgers, Mike Piazza (40), Eric Karros (31), Todd Zeile (31), and Raul Mondesi (30) each topped 30 home runs, but no other player on the team made it to double-figures and the Dodgers hit just 174 homers. The 1995 Colorado Rockies almost joined the Dodgers. They had four players break the 30-homer mark – Dante Bichette (40), Larry Walker (36), Vinny Castilla (32) and Andres Galarraga (31) – and they finished with exactly 200 homers. Entering the season's final game with 198 homers, the Rockies got their final two homers of the year in the third inning of their 10-9 win over the Giants at Coors Field. Eric Young and Larry Walker each hit two-run shots against Joe Rosselli – the final two homers given up by Rosselli in his nine-game career.

Ellis Burks, with 14 round-trippers, was the only other Rockie to reach double-figures.

In 1987 the Detroit Tigers squeaked by the Toronto Blue Jays by two games to win the American League East title. The Blue Jay nipped the Tigers 10-9 on September 26 at Toronto on a three-run, bases-loaded triple in the bottom of the ninth by pinch-hitter Juan Beniquez. The stunning comeback gave Toronto a lead of 3 1/2 games with a week to play. Detroit cut the lead back to 2 1/2 games the next day with a grueling 3-2 win in 13 innings. Toronto then lost their next three against Milwaukee to limp into a season-ending, three-game series at Detroit with a one-game lead. Detroit pulled even in the standings with a 4-3 win in the first game and then took a one-game lead when they won the next game 3-2 on Alan Trammell's twelfth-inning single. With Toronto needing a victory in the season's final game to force a one-game playoff, Jimmy Key allowed the Tigers just three hits but lost 1-0 due to Larry Herndon's homer in the second. During the season the two teams met 13 times – with 11 of the games, including the *last four* Detroit wins, being decided by one run.

The 2004 New York Yankees are the only team to win 100 games without a 15-game winner on their pitching staff. The Yanks won 101 games and were led by Javier Vazquez and Jon Lieber (14 wins each), Mike Mussina (12) and Kevin Brown (10). Three other teams won 100 or more games with no pitcher getting more than 15 victories. The 1941 Yankees won 101 games with Lefty Gomez and Red Ruffing tying for a team-high 15 wins. In 1975 the Cincinnati Reds won 108 games with *three pitchers* – Gary Nolan, Jack Billingham, and Don Gullett – winning a team-high 15 games. The next season Cincinnati won 102 games and had seven pitchers record double-digit win totals, but only Gary Nolan reached the 15-win mark.

The Washington Senators managed only *one* home run at their home field in 1945 – and it *did not* leave the park. In their 135th game of the year, the Senators finally homered at Griffith Stadium when Joe Kuhel hit a solo inside-the-park homer against Bob Muncrief in the third inning of their 3-2 win against the Browns on September

7. Washington's other 26 homers came at Comiskey Park (7), Sportsman's Park (5), Tiger Stadium (4), Fenway Park (3), Yankee Stadium (3), Shibe Park (2), Cleveland Stadium (1) and League Park (1). Harlond Clift led the team with the last eight of his 178 career homers, including the last three of his career in a doubleheader on July 4 at Comiskey Park. George Myatt, Fred Vaughn, Mike Kreevich, and Rick Ferrell each homered once – *the last career homer for each of them* – and Hillis Layne also homered once, his only career homer. The Senators' seven homers at Comiskey Park (in only 11 games) was *just one less* than the 1945 White Sox hit in their home ballpark in 74 games.

On April 8, 1969, four new teams made their debut – *each winning by a single run.* The Montreal Expos gave up four runs in the bottom of the ninth but held on to beat the Mets 11-10 at Shea Stadium. The Kansas City Royals nipped the Minnesota Twins 4-3 in 12 innings with a one-out, bases-loaded, pinch-hit single by Joe Keough which came against Twins' pitcher Dick Woodson who was making his major league debut. The San Diego Padres took a 2-1 home win over the Houston Astros in their first game with Dick Selma pitching a complete game while giving up just five hits and striking out 12. The Seattle Pilots, in their only season before moving to Milwaukee and becoming the Brewers, got a two-run homer from Mike Hegan as they plated four runs in the top of the first inning and held on to beat the Angels 4-3.

The 1936 New York Yankees are the only team to have five players with 100 or more RBIs. Lou Gehrig led the way with 152 RBIs, followed by Joe DiMaggio (125), Tony Lazzeri (109), Bill Dickey (107) and George Selkirk (107).

In 1997 the Colorado Rockies finished 83-79 to become the only team to finish above .500 *despite not having a pitcher win ten games.* Roger Bailey (9-10 in 29 starts) and Darren Holmes (9-2 in 42 games, including six starts) led the team in wins, followed by Jamey Wright (8-12) and John Thomson (7-9). Bailey won his ninth game on July 26, but then went 0-3 with eight no-decisions in his last 11 starts. The Rockies used 23 different pitchers during the season with 18 of them winning at least one game.

The last game in the history of the Washington Senators was a forfeit to the New York Yankees at Robert F. Kennedy Stadium on September 30, 1971. The Senators led the Yankees 7-5 with two outs and nobody on base when hundreds of fans, angry at Washington owner Bob Short's decision to move the team to Texas for the 1972 season, stormed the field and began roaming around the outfield and ripping up the bases. According to baseball rules, the Yankees were awarded a 9-0 victory. All of the individual statistics counted, but there was not a winning or losing pitcher.

The longest losing streak in the history of the Chicago Cubs is also the longest losing streak to begin a season by a National League team. The Cubs started the 1997 season by dropping their first 14 games before finally getting in the win column on April 20 with a 4-3 win in the second game of a doubleheader against the Mets at Shea Stadium. The Baltimore Orioles set the major league record when they dropped 21 games in a row to start the 1988 season.

In a wild game on July 24, 1998, the Phillies rallied in their last at-bat in *four consecutive innings* before finally beating the Florida Marlins 7-6 at Veterans Stadium. After taking the first game of the doubleheader 6-4 on Scott Rolen's homer in the 12th, Philadelphia was trailing 3-1 in the bottom of the ninth inning of the second game when Mark Lewis hit a two-out, two-run homer to tie it. Florida regained the lead in the 10th on a homer by Craig Counsell only to let the Phillies retie the game on shortstop Dave Berg's throwing error with two outs. In the 11th Florida took the lead again on a single by Cliff Floyd, but Philadelphia loaded the bases in the bottom of the frame with one out. They tied the game at 5-5 on a walk to Kevin Sefcik, but then Mark Parent grounded into a double play to end the inning. Todd Zeile's single to left scored Mike Redmond in the 12th and gave the Marlins another lead at 6-5, but the Phillies rallied one last time. Ruben Amaro led off the last of the 12th and quickly tied the game again by homering on the second pitch against Vic Darensbourg. Following a single, sacrifice bunt, and intentional walk, Rico Brogna singled in Doug Glanville to win the game.

Triples

The 1981 San Diego Padres are the last team to hit more triples than home runs in a season. In the strike-plagued season of 1981, the Padres smacked 35 triples and just 32 homers in 110 games. They were led in triples by Gene Richards (12) and in home runs by Joe Lefebvre (8). The last American League team to accomplish this feat is the 1949 Chicago White Sox who ended up with 66 triples and only 43 homers. The White Sox had 21 different players collect at least one triple, led by Cass Michaels with nine, Dave Philley with eight, and Chuck Kress who had six. Bud Souchock topped the team in home runs with seven and Michaels chipped in six.

From 1991 to 1994, Lance Johnson of the Chicago White Sox led or tied for the American League lead in triples each season. Johnson made a late-season run at the AL triples title in 1995 when he went 6-6 with a record-tying three triples on September 23 against the Twins. He added another one the next day to tie Kenny Lofton for the AL lead, but Lofton deprived Johnson of a fifth straight league-leading season by coming up with a triple the last day of the season – his first triple since he slapped two on August 16. Johnson moved over to the National League's New York Mets in 1996 and led the NL with 21 triples, the most in the NL since 1930. If not for Lofton's triple on the final day of 1995, Johnson would have led the league in triples for six consecutive years.

Brett Butler led the league in triples *with three different teams.* Butler paced the National League with 13 triples for the 1983 Atlanta

Braves and topped the American League with 14 triples with the 1986 Cleveland Indians. Eight years later he tied for the National League lead with nine triples in 1994 while with the Los Angeles Dodgers and led again in 1995 when he split time between the Dodgers and the New York Mets. Following the 1997 season, Butler retired with 131 career triples.

Mark McGwire hammered 583 home runs but hit just six career triples. McGwire collected his four triples in 1987 and another on June 20, 1988, against Milwaukee's Teddy Higuera at County Stadium. He then batted a major league record 4,618 times before hitting his last triple on August 2, 1999, against San Diego's Trevor Hoffman.

Rickey Henderson used his great speed and baserunning skills to set records of 1,406 stolen bases and 2,295 runs scored. However, Hendeson never hit more than seven triples in any season and had only 66 three-baggers in his 23-year big league career.

During the 2000 season, Dave Martinez achieved the unique feat of hitting a triple for four different teams in one season. He tripled twice for Tampa Bay (April 13 and 20) and once each for the Chicago Cubs (May 17), Texas (July 8) and Toronto (September 20).

In the strike-shortened 1994 season, Sammy Sosa tripled six times in 426 at-bats – *with four of them coming in consecutive games at Wrigley Field within a span of 14 at-bats.* Sosa collected three-baggers on May 14 and 15 against Florida and on May 16 and 17 against San Diego.

Trenidad Hubbard legged out just seven triples in his ten-year career – *but had triples with six different clubs.* Hubbard's first two three-baggers were for Colorado (July 19, 1994, and April 15, 1996) at Coors Field, and he also tripled for San Francisco (August 25, 1996), Los Angeles (August 3, 1998), Atlanta (May 21, 2000), Baltimore (August 2, 2000), and Kansas City (May 6, 2001).

During his long career the only offensive category in which Hall of Fame catcher Carlton Fisk led the American League was *triples*. In 1972, his first full year in the majors, Fisk tied Oakland's Joe Rudi with nine triples.

From 1977 to 1996, Eddie Murray had one, two, or three triples per season, except for the 1995 season when he failed to hit a three-bagger. Although he did not triple in the 1995 regular season, Murray did triple against Boston's Erik Hanson in Game 2 of the Division Series.

Two of a Kind

Two players have gotten three hits in one inning – *both of them with the Boston Red Sox at Fenway Park*. Gene Stephens was the first to do it on June 18, 1953, when Boston beat the Detroit Tigers 22-3, highlighted by a major league single-inning record of 17 runs in the seventh inning. Despite hitting just .204 (45 for 221) in 1953, Stephens singled to right field against Steve Gromek, doubled to center against Dick Weik, and slapped another single to right against Earl Harrist. The Red Sox began their June 27, 2003, game against the Florida Marlins by setting a major league record of scoring ten runs before making an out. Johnny Damon started the assault with a double to right against Carl Pavano, followed with a triple to center against Michael Tejera and then a single to left off Allen Levrault. Boston's first-inning explosion tied the American League record for most runs in the first inning of a game with 14, just one away from the major league mark set by Brooklyn in 1952. Ironically, Damon's third hit ended Boston's big inning because Bill Mueller attempted to score and was thrown out at the plate, preventing them from tying Brooklyn's record.

Bob Grim and Pedro Martinez are the only two pitchers to win 20 games while pitching fewer than 200 innings. Grim, a rookie with the 1954 Yankees, appeared in 37 games (including 20 starts) and was 20-6 with an ERA of 3.26 and a career-high 108 strikeouts in only 199 innings. Martinez pitched 199.1 innings in 30 starts for the 2002 Boston Red Sox and ended up 20-4 with a 2.26 ERA and 239 strikeouts.

In a 15-5 win over the New York Yankees at Cleveland Stadium on April 8, 1993, Indians' second baseman Carlos Baerga became the first player to homer from both sides of the plate in one inning. In the bottom of the seventh inning, he hit a two-run homer against southpaw Steve Howe and after the Indians batted around he hit a solo homer off righthander Steve Farr. Mark Bellhorn of the Chicago Cubs matched Baerga's feat on August 29, 2002, during a 13-10 Cubs' victory over the Milwaukee Brewers at Miller Park. He homered from the right side of the plate against Andrew Lorraine and from the left side against Jose Cabrera in the Cubs' ten-run fourth inning.

Jimmie Foxx and Mark McGwire are the only players to hit 50 home runs in a season for two different teams. Foxx smacked 58 long balls for the Philadelphia A's in 1932 and another 50 for the Boston Red Sox in 1938. McGwire hammered 52 homers for Oakland in 1996 and followed that with 58 more in 1997 while splitting time between Oakland and St. Louis. In his first full season with the Cardinals in 1998, McGwire became the first major leaguer to reach the 70-homer mark, and he then cranked 65 more for St. Louis in 1999.

Darrell Evans and Reggie Jackson are the only players to hit at least 100 home runs for three different clubs. Evans did it for the Braves (131), Giants (142) and Tigers (141), Jackson pulled it off with the A's (268), Yankees (144), and Angels (123).

Red Rolfe and Doc Cramer are the only two players to collect ten hits in a single World Series without getting an extra-base hit. Rolfe had ten singles for the New York Yankees in the 1936 World Series while Cramer had 11 singles for the Detroit Tigers in the 1945 Series.

Only two teams have started a game with the first three batters hitting home runs. The San Diego Padres were the first to do it on April 13, 1987, when Marvell Wynne, Tony Gwynn, and John Kruk homered in succession to open the bottom of the first against San Francisco's Roger Mason. Despite the Padres' early outburst, the Giants rallied to win the game 13-6. Wynne would homer just once more during the 1987 season. The second team to do it was the Atlanta Braves on May 28, 2003. Rafael Furcal, Mark DeRosa and Gary Sheffield each began the game with a homer against Cincinnati's Jeff Austin on their way to a 15-3 win at Turner Field. Chipper Jones had ended the previous game by hitting a home run in the bottom of the 10th against Chris Reitsma, so the Braves' explosion against Austin also tied the major league team record of four consecutive homers.

Nine pitchers have appeared in more than 1,000 games, but John Franco (90-87, 424 saves in 1,119 games) and Kent Tekulve (94-90, 184 saves in 1,050 games) are the only two who never started a game in their career.

Only two pitchers have won 240 games without the benefit of a 20-win season. Dennis Martinez compiled a career mark of 245-193 from 1976 to 1998, ending his 23-year big league career with exactly 4,000 innings pitched. His career best in wins was 16, which he did twice with Baltimore (1978 and 1982) and twice with Montreal (1989 and 1992). Frank Tanana won 240 and lost 236 games from 1973 to 1993. His best season was 19-10 with the California Angels in 1976.

Hank Borowy (1945) and Bartolo Colon (2002) are the only pitchers to win ten games in each league during one season. Borowy was 10-5 for the Yankees before being sold to the Cubs on July 27. He went 11-2 with the Cubs to finish the year at 21-7. Colon was 10-4 for the Indians before being traded on June 27 to the Expos. where he also went 10-4 to finish with a 20-8 record.

Jack Kubiszyn and Odalis Perez are the only two players to hit their only career home run in a 1-0 game. Kubiszyn, whose career lasted just 50 games and 101 at-bats with Cleveland, homered off Kansas City's Bill Fischer in the seventh inning on August 3, 1962, at Municipal Stadium. Perez pitched Los Angeles to a victory at Dodger Stadium on August 28, 2002, when he hurled eight scoreless innings and accounted for the only run with a blast in the bottom of the fifth against Arizona's Rick Helling.

Alfredo Griffin and Paul O'Neill are the only two players to appear in three perfect games. Griffin was on the losing side each time while O'Neill's team won each game. Griffin was the leadoff hitter for the Toronto when Len Barker retired all 27 Blue Jays he faced on May 15, 1981. Griffin and O'Neill crossed paths during Tom Browning's perfect game against Los Angeles on September 16, 1988, with Griffin batting leadoff for the Dodgers and O'Neill playing right field for Cincinnati. Griffin was still with the Dodgers when they had another perfect game pitched against them on July 28, 1991, this time by Montreal's Dennis Martinez. Ten years after his first one, O'Neill played in two perfect games at Yankee Stadium. He was the Yankees' right fielder during David Wells' gem against Minnesota on May 17, 1998, and David Cone's masterpiece against Montreal on July 18, 1999.

Since 1900 only two pitchers have won 20 games in a season while having an ERA over 5.00. Ray Kremer was 20-12 with a 5.02 ERA for the Pittsburgh Pirates in 1930 and Bobo Newsom compiled a record of 20-16 with an ERA of 5.08 for the St. Louis Browns in 1938.

Mark McGwire hit 58 home runs in 1997 while splitting the season between the Cardinals and A's but scored only 86 runs, making him the first player with 50-home run season to score fewer than 100 times. Atlanta's Andruw Jones joined McGwire in 2005 when he scored just 95 runs while hitting 51 homers.

Johnny Mize and Dave Kingman are the only sluggers to hit three home runs in a game with three different teams. Mize, along with Sammy Sosa, holds the record for most three-home run games, doing it six times in his career. He accomplished the feat four times for the St. Louis Cardinals (twice in 1938 and twice in 1940), with the New York Giants (1947), and with the New York Yankees (1950).

Kingman had his three-homer games for the New York Mets (1976), Chicago Cubs (1978 and twice in 1979) and Oakland A's (1984).

Ty Cobb and Rusty Staub are the only players to homer before their twentieth birthday *and* after their fortieth birthday. Cobb hit one home run in both 1905 and 1906 before turning 20 on December 18, 1906, and swatted five round-trippers for the Philadelphia A's in 1927 and one more in 1928 after turning 40. Staub was born on April 1, 1944, and homered six times for Houston in 1963 and once for the New York Mets in both 1984 and 1985.

World Series and Playoffs

Frankie Frisch is one of eight players to play in at least 50 World Series games – *but the only one to do it without playing for the Yankees.* Frisch played in exactly 50 games, spread over eight World Series. He was a member of the New York Giants during their run of four consecutive National League pennants from 1921 to 1924 and was with the St. Louis Cardinals when they took the NL flag in 1928, 1930, 1931, and 1934. Frisch's teams were 4-4 in World Series action, winning championships in his first two and last two Series appearances. During his 50 World Series games, Frisch never connected for a home run and still holds the record for most World Series at-bats (197) without a homer.

David Justice was on the losing side of three World Series that ended in the home team's last at-bat of Game 7. Justice was with Atlanta in the 1991 World Series when the Braves were beaten 1-0 by Minnesota in the bottom of the 10th by Gene Larkin's hit that scored Dan Gladden. In the 1997 World Series, Justice was with Cleveland, seeking their first title since 1948, when an 11th-inning single by Florida's Edgar Renteria scored Craig Counsell to beat them 3-2. Justice also played with the New York Yankees in the 2001 World Series, which ended in the bottom of the ninth with Luis Gonzalez blooping a single to short left-center field to score Jay Bell and win the game 3-2.

Lonnie Smith was the first player to bat in a playoff game in Canada – *for both the National League and the American League.*

Baseball's first playoff game outside the U.S. was played in Montreal on October 7, 1981, and Smith was the Phillies' leadoff batter in Game 1 against Expos' pitcher Steve Rogers. The first American League playoff game played outside the U.S. took place on October 8, 1985, and Smith led off Game 1 for the Royals as they took on Dave Stieb and the Blue Jays in Toronto.

Kirk Gibson homered dramatically in his last two World Series at-bats – *which were four years apart.* In Game 5 of the 1984 World Series, Gibson launched a three-run homer in the eighth inning against Goose Gossage to secure Detroit's victory over San Diego. Four years later, in his only at-bat in the 1988 Series, an injured Gibson limped to the plate in the bottom of the ninth and hit an unforgettable pinch-hit home run against Dennis Eckersley to win Game 1 to propel Los Angeles to a five-game World Series victory over Oakland.

After not appearing in a World Series in his first 16 years, Don Baylor ended his career by playing in three consecutive World Series – *each time with a different team.* Baylor played in four games for Boston in the 1986 Series and was 2 for 11 with an RBI. The next year with Minnesota, Baylor got into five games was 5 for 13 with a home run and three RBIs. His major league career ended the next season when he failed in a single pinch-hit attempt for Oakland in the 1988 Series. Despite appearing in ten of the 19 World Series games from 1986 to 1988, Baylor did not appear in the most memorable game of each Series. His name is not in the box score of Game 6 ("the Bill Buckner game") in 1986, the Jack Morris 1-0, ten-inning win over Atlanta in Game 7 in 1991 or Game 1 in 1988 that ended with Kirk Gibson's dramatic home run off Dennis Eckersley.

In the 1988 World Series against the Los Angeles Dodgers, Oakland's Jose Canseco and Mark McGwire hit a combined 2 for 36, but each smacked a home run. In the top of the second of Game 1, Canseco hit a grand slam against Tim Belcher in his first official World Series at-bat (after being hit by a pitch in his first plate appearance). McGwire won Game 3 at Oakland with a solo home run in the bottom of the ninth off Jay Howell.

Cleveland's Carlos Baerga made the last out in three of the four Indians' losses in the 1995 World Series. He popped out to third baseman Chipper Jones to end Games 1 and 2 and flied out to center fielder Marquis Grissom to end the Series in Game 6.

Detroit Tiger pitcher Mickey Lolich never hit a home run in the regular season in 821 at-bats – *but hit one in Game 2 of the 1968 World Series.* Lolich connected in the third inning against St. Louis Cardinals' pitcher Nelson Briles for a solo home run at Busch Stadium as the Tigers beat the Cardinals 8-1. He is the only player to hit his only career home run in the World Series.

The two largest shutouts in playoff or World Series history occurred within a three-game span between the same teams. Down three games to one in the NLCS, Atlanta beat St. Louis 14-0 in Game 5 on October 14, 1996, and then pulled even with the Cardinals with a 3-1 win behind Greg Maddux in Game 6. They wrapped up the NL pennant and advanced to the World Series by pounding the Cardinals 15-0 in Game 7.

Tied at two games each in the World Series, Brooklyn and Cleveland met at Cleveland's League Park for Game 5 on October 10, 1920, and produced three significant "firsts". Elmer Smith staked the Indians to a quick lead in the bottom of the first when he smashed a pitch from Burleigh Grimes for the first World Series grand slam. In the fourth inning, the Indians' starting pitcher Jim Bagby hit a three-run homer against Grimes, becoming the first pitcher to hit a World Series home run. In the fifth the Dodgers threatened with two men on and no outs, but Indians' second baseman Bill Wambsganss snared pitcher Clarence Mitchell's line drive and turned it into an unassisted triple play – the only triple play in World Series history. Mitchell would also hit into a double play in the seventh, accounting for five outs in two at-bats.

On October 20, 1996, at Yankee Stadium, 19-year-old Andruw Jones of the Atlanta Braves hit homers the first two times he batted in the World Series, matching the feat of Oakland's Gene Tenace in the 1972 World Series. Jones' historic homers also broke Mickey

Mantle's record as the youngest player to homer in the World Series – and came on the 65th anniversary of Mantle's birth.

Terry Pendleton played on five losing World Series teams – *without ever being a member of a World Series champion.* Pendleton was a member of the 1985 and 1987 St. Louis Cardinals as well as the 1991, 1992, and 1996 Atlanta Braves. He missed out on the Braves' 1995 championship because he spent that year with the Florida Marlins before being traded back to Atlanta on August 13, 1996.

From 1991 to 2004, the Atlanta Braves lost in the National League playoffs eight times – *each time to a different team.* They lost to Philadelphia (1993), Florida (1997), San Diego (1998), St. Louis (2000), Arizona (2001), San Francisco (2002), Chicago (2003) and Houston (2004). Including their World Series appearances since 1991, the Braves lost a total of 12 times to 11 different teams – they were beaten in World Series play by Minnesota (1991), Toronto (1992) and New York (1996 and 1999).

Alejandro Pena was the winning pitcher in Game 1 of the 1988 World Series when the Dodgers' Kirk Gibson hit his dramatic pinch-hitter home run against Dennis Eckersley to beat Oakland 5-4. Pena was also the losing pitcher in Game 7 of the 1991 World Series, the classic 1-0, ten-inning Minnesota victory over Atlanta.

The Minnesota Twins have a World Series record of 11-1 at home – but have yet to win a World Series road game, going 0-9 in three World Series. The Twins lost the 1965 World Series to Los Angeles, losing Game 7 at home after winning the first three home games and losing three at Dodger Stadium. In 1987 the Twins beat the St. Louis Cardinals and became the first team to win a World Series by winning all four games at home, a feat they duplicated just four years later when they beat the Braves in the 1991 World Series.

The Boston Red Sox have appeared in four World Series in four different decades since 1946, and each time they faced the National League team with the best regular season record of that decade. Boston lost seven-game Series to the 1967 St. Louis Cardinals (101 wins), 1975 Cincinnati Reds (108 wins) and the 1986 New York Mets (108 wins). The Red Sox ended their 86-year World Series drought in 2004 with a sweep of the St. Louis Cardinals (105 wins, the most in the 2000s so far). During their sweep in 2004, Boston joined the 1963 Dodgers, 1966 Orioles and 1989 A's as the only teams to never trail at *any time* in a World Series sweep.

New York Yankees' pitcher Ralph Terry was the losing pitcher in Game 7 of the 1960 World Series against Pittsburgh when he gave up Bill Mazeroski's famous home run. He was also the winning pitcher of Game 7 of the 1962 World Series against San Francisco when he got Willie McCovey to line out viscously to second base to end the game with runners on second and third and the score 1-0.

The 1987 Minnesota Twins are the only World Series champions to be outscored in the regular season. Despite scoring only 786 runs while allowing 806, the Twins finished the 1987 regular season with a record of 85-77, two games ahead of Kansas City in the AL West and then shocked the favored Tigers in the ALCS and beat St. Louis in seven games for the title. Their .525 winning percentage is the lowest ever for a World Series champion.

St. Louis Cardinals' shortstop Ozzie Smith homered against Los Angeles Dodgers' pitcher Tom Niedenfuer in the bottom of the ninth to win Game 5 of the 1985 National League Championship Series. Smith's dramatic ninth-inning blast was his first career homer from the left side of the plate and the only home run he hit in 144 playoff and World Series at-bats.

Bob Gibson pitched in nine World Series games for the St. Louis Cardinals, compiling a 7-2 record. Gibson lost his first World Series start against the New York Yankees on October 8, 1964, but then won seven consecutive World Series games before losing to the Detroit Tigers in Game 7 of the 1968 World Series. Gibson completed eight of his nine World Series starts, including a ten-inning win in Game 5 of the 1964 Series. The only game that Gibson did not go the distance was his first game in which he went eight innings.

Among players who hit at least four home runs in a single World Series, Lou Gehrig is the only player who did it in a four-game Series. During the Yankees' sweep of the St. Louis Cardinals in the 1928 Series, Gehrig connected for a three-run homer in Game 2, a solo blast and a two-run homer in Game 3 and another solo shot in Game 4. Despite his four homers (plus a single and a double), Gehrig was overshadowed by his teammate Babe Ruth who collected ten hits in 16 at-bats, including three home runs in Game 4.

The two highest-scoring games in the history of the World Series are Game 4 of the 1993 Series when Toronto topped Philadelphia 15-14 and Game 3 of the 1997 Series when Florida beat Cleveland 14-11. Although the games were played four years apart and four different clubs were involved, five players appeared in both games. In the 1993 game, Devon White, Tony Fernandez, and Al Leiter appeared for the Blue Jays and Darren Daulton and Jim Eisenreich participated for the Phillies. Four years later, White, Leiter, Daulton, and Eisenreich were members of the Marlins and Fernandez was with the Indians.

Reggie Jackson secured his spot in World Series history by hitting three consecutive home runs (each time on the first pitch) against Los Angeles in Game 6 of the 1977 Series – *but Jackson actually homered on four consecutive swings*. In his last at-bat of Game 5 at LA, Jackson homered against Don Sutton in the eighth inning. Back at Yankee Stadium for Game 6, Jackson walked on four pitches against Burt Hooton in the second inning, and then homered on the first pitch from Hooton in the fourth, Elias Sosa in the fifth, and Charlie Hough in the eighth. Jackson also homered in his third at-bat of Game 1 of the 1978 World Series, giving him five homers in seven at-bats over three World Series games.

The Baltimore Orioles are the only team to hit ten home runs in a World Series that lasted fewer than seven games. Brooks Robinson, Frank Robinson and Boog Powell each hit two homers, as the Orioles swatted ten home runs when they won the 1970 Series against the Cincinnati Reds in five games. The New York Yankees socked ten homers in the World Series four times (1952, 1958, 1960, and 1964) and smacked 12 in the 1956 Series, but in each case they did it in a seven-game Series. The San Francisco Giants, the only NL team to hit ten or more long balls in a World Series, belted a record 14 World Series homers in 2002 – *but still lost to Anaheim in seven games.* Barry Bonds clubbed four home runs and Jeff Kent added three more, but eight of San Francisco's homers came in their losses in Games 2, 3, and 6. They did not homer in Game 7 and lost 4-1.

In the 1926 World Series, the New York Yankees lost in seven games to the St. Louis Cardinals. The Yankees hit four homers in the Series, all by Babe Ruth. The only other instance of a player hitting all of his team's World Series home runs (minimum of three homers) occurred in the 1979 World Series when Willie Stargell hit three for Pittsburgh and led the Pirates to a seven-game victory over the Baltimore Orioles.

Larry Jansen was the winning pitcher for the New York Giants when Bobby Thomson hit his dramatic home run on October 3, 1951, to beat the Brooklyn Dodgers. The victory was his 23rd of the season, tying Jansen for the National League lead with his teammate Sal Maglie, who had started the game and left following the eighth inning, having allowed four runs. Jansen was summoned from the bullpen with the Dodgers up 4-1, retired the Dodgers in order in the top of the ninth and then became the winner when Thomson's home run rallied the Giants past the Dodgers 5-4.

John Wetteland is the only pitcher to save four games in a single World Series. Wetteland appeared in five games in the 1996 Series for New York, saving the final four games of their six-game victory over the Braves. He pitched a total of 4.1 innings, allowing four hits and striking out six Braves.

In ten American League Championship Series games, Dave Stewart had a record of 8-0 with a 2.03 ERA. Pitching for the Oakland A's, Stewart won Game 4 of the 1988 ALCS against Boston, Games 1 and 5 of the 1989 ALCS against Toronto, Games 1 and 4 of the 1990 ALCS against Boston, and Game 5 of the 1992

ALCS against Toronto. In the 1993 ALCS, Stewart pitched for Toronto and was the winning pitcher in Games 2 and 6 against the Chicago White Sox.

Mickey Mantle set three World Series batting records *with his last World Series hit*. Mantle smacked a three-run homer against Bob Gibson in the sixth inning of Game 7 of the 1964 World Series. The long ball was his 18th World Series home run, extending his own record, and gave him 40 RBIs and 42 runs scored in World Series play, breaking the records set by his former teammate Yogi Berra.

The Baltimore Orioles scored just 13 runs in the 1966 World Series yet swept Los Angeles because they held the Dodgers to just *two runs* for the entire Series. The Dodgers scored single runs in the second and third innings of Game 1 – both charged to Dave McNally – and then were blanked for 33 consecutive innings. Moe Drabowsky shut down the LA hitters for the final 6.2 innings of Game 1 and the Orioles held on to win 5-2. In the next three games, the Dodgers were shut out 6-0 by Jim Palmer, 1-0 by Wally Bunker and 1-0 by McNally, with each of the Oriole hurlers going the distance.

George Frazier lost three games in the 1981 World Series. Frazier gave up nine hits and seven earned runs in 3.2 relief innings for an ERA of 17.18 and was the losing pitcher in Games 3, 4 and 6 to the Los Angeles Dodgers, who overcame a two-game deficit to win the Series. The only other instance of a pitcher losing three games in a World Series occurred in 1919 when Chicago White Sox pitcher Claude "Lefty" Williams – one of the eight players charged with conspiring to fix the 1919 World Series – lost three times to the Cincinnati Reds.

Jim Kaat holds the record for longest span between World Series appearances. Kaat played in three games for the Minnesota Twins in the 1965 Series against the Los Angeles Dodgers, winning in Game 2 and taking the loss in Games 5 and 7, as the Dodgers beat the Twins for the championship. Kaat's only other Fall Classic appearance was not until 1982 when he pitched for the St. Louis Cardinals against the Milwaukee Brewers. He pitched in each of the first four games of the Series, totaling 2.1 innings, but did not receive a decision.

When Atlanta Braves' second baseman Mark Lemke tripled three times in the 1991 World Series, he was the first player to do so since the New York Yankees' Billy Johnson smacked three in 1947. The only other players to get at least three triples in a World Series all did so in the first modern World Series in 1903. Boston Red Sox players Buck Freeman, Freddy Parent, and Chick Stahl each hit three triples, and Tommy Leach belted a World Series record four three-baggers for the Pittsburgh Pirates.

The 1905 World Series is the only Series in which each game was a shutout. Behind the pitching of ace Christy Mathewson, the New York Giants beat the Philadelphia A's in five games. The Series opened in Philadelphia with Mathewson going the distance, giving up only four hits and fanning six batters, as the Giants won 3-0. The A's rallied behind the complete-game, nine-strikeout performance of Chief Bender to win Game 2 in New York by the score of 3-0. Mathewson returned in Game 3 at Philadelphia and shut out the A's 9-0, pitching nine innings with eight whiffs and allowing only four hits. New York returned home and took Game 4 behind the pitching of Joe McGinity who allowed five hits and went the distance, edging A's hurler Eddie Plank 1-0. The Giants then took Game 5 by a 2-0 score behind a nine-inning, six-hit performance by Mathewson. For the Series, Mathewson was 3-0 and allowed just 14 hits and one walk, while striking out 18, in 27 innings of work.

Despite an ERA of 0.95 with 61 strikeouts in 57 innings of work in the World Series, Sandy Koufax's record in eight World Series games was just 4-3. After two hitless innings of relief in Game 1 of the 1959 World Series against the Chicago White Sox, Koufax started Game 5 and was the loser despite giving up only one run in seven innings. Koufax notched two wins in the 1963 World Series when he beat Whitey Ford and the Yankees in Games 1 and 4. Both wins were complete games and he allowed only three earned runs. In the first encounter against Ford, Koufax fanned Harry Bright to end the game and break Carl Erskine's record of 14 strikeouts in a World Series game, a mark since topped by Bob Gibson. In his first game of the 1965 Series, Koufax lost Game 2 to Minnesota's Jim Kaat despite whiffing nine and giving up just one earned run in six innings. He rebounded to lead the Dodgers to the title by winning Games 5 and 7 – each a ten-strikeout, complete-game shutout. In his final major league start, Game 2 of the 1966 World Series against Baltimore, Koufax allowed just one earned run, but the Dodger defense let him down by committing six errors, which led to three unearned runs. He lost 6-0 to 20-year-old Jim Palmer, the youngest pitcher to shut out an opponent in the World Series.

In the 1986 season, Steve Crawford did not win a regular season game for the Boston Red Sox – *but he won one game in the both ALCS and the World Series.* Crawford appeared in 40 regular season games and compiled a record of 0-2 with four saves in 57.1 innings of relief. In Game 5 of the ALCS, California rallied to retie the game in the bottom of the ninth after Dave Henderson's dramatic home run against Donnie Moore in the top of the inning had given the Red Sox a one-run lead. Crawford entered the game in the bottom of the ninth with the bases loaded and just one out. He worked out of the jam, pitched a scoreless 10th, and was the winner when the Sox scored in the top of the 11th and held on to win. In the Game 2 of the World Series, Crawford was the winning pitcher in Boston's victory over the New York Mets. With one out in the fifth and the Red Sox ahead 6-2, Crawford entered the game in relief of Roger Clemens and pitched 1.2 innings, allowing one hit and striking out two batters. Boston held on win 9-3 and Crawford was awarded the win because the starter Clemens failed to pitch the necessary five innings to qualify for the victory.

Don Newcombe was a three-time 20-game winner for the Brooklyn Dodgers but was 0-4 with an 8.59 ERA in the World Series. Following his rookie season, Newcombe pitched well and fanned 11 in Game 1 of the 1949 World Series but was a 1-0 loser when he surrendered a solo home run to New York's Tommy Henrich in the bottom of the ninth. Newcombe also lost Game 4, giving up three earned runs while lasting just 3.2 innings. Brooklyn beat the Yankees in 1955 to win their only championship, but Newcombe lost the opener by giving up six earned runs in 5.2 innings. Coming off a 27-win season and winning the first Cy Young Award, Newcombe was again roughed up by the Yankees in the 1956 World Series. He started Game 2 and allowed six earned runs in just 1.2 innings but got a no-decision because the Dodgers rallied to win. The Series went seven games, and Newcombe was the loser in the deciding game after surrendering five runs in three innings.

Orel Hershiser is the only player to win the MVP award in both the NLCS and the ALCS. Hershiser ended the 1988 season by throwing a major league record 59 consecutive innings and then led the Los Angeles Dodgers to a seven-game NLCS victory over the favored New York Mets by appearing in four games, recording a win and a save. Coming off a season in which they had a 10-1 record against the Dodgers in the regular season, the Mets won the first game by the score of 3-2. Hershiser pitched 8.1 innings, allowing just two earned runs and striking out six, but got a no-decision. In Game 3 he gave up just one earned run in seven innings and again got a no-decision as the Mets won 8-4. Hershisher was summoned from the bullpen in Game 4 and sealed the Dodgers' 5-4 win by getting Kevin McReynolds to pop out to center field with the bases loaded and two away in the ninth. After New York rallied to tie the series at three games each, Hershiser went the distance in Game 7 and shut out the Mets 6-0 on just five hits and advanced the Dodgers into the World Series. In the 1995 ALCS, he threw a combined 14 innings, allowed just two earned runs and struck out 15. He was the winner of Games 2 and 5 as Cleveland advanced to their first World Series since 1954.

Bucky Harris managed two teams to World Series championships – and they came 23 years apart. Harris was the 27-year-old player-manager of the Washington Senators in 1924 and guided them to their only World Series championship. Despite just one regular season home run in 143 games, he hit two in the Series while batting .333 (11 for 33) with seven RBIs. His fourth-inning homer against

Virgil Barnes in Game 7 accounted for Washington's first run in their 4-3, 12-inning win that gave them a World Series triumph over the New York Giants. Harris was also at the helm of the New York Yankees in 1947 when they beat the Brooklyn Dodgers in seven games. Despite two World Series titles, Harris finished his 29-year managerial career with a losing record of 2,157-2,218.

Among the teams that have appeared in more than one World Series, the Toronto Blue Jays and Florida Marlins are the only ones with a perfect record. Each franchise has a 2-0 World Series record. The Blue Jays defeated Atlanta in 1992 and Philadelphia in 1993. Florida beat Cleveland in 1997 and New York in 2003.

In the 1999 NLCS against New York, the Atlanta Braves set the record for the most runners left on base in a playoff or World Series game – *just one day after they left nobody on base*. The Braves lost Game 4 by a score of 3-2 and had only three baserunners, Bret Boone who singled and was caught stealing in the fourth and Brian Jordan and Ryan Klesko who homered back-to-back in the eighth. The next night New York edged the Braves 4-3 in 15 innings with the Braves leaving 19 men on base. The Mets managed to win despite not scoring for *13 consecutive innings*. After getting two runs in the first the Mets would not score again until the bottom of the 15th when, with Atlanta leading 3-2, New York rallied to tie the game and had the bases loaded with one out. Robin Ventura hit what should have been a grand slam to win the game but was only credited with an RBI single because he was mobbed by his teammates near second base and never made it around to touch home plate.

After winning Game 5 of the 1986 World Series against the New York Mets, the Boston Red Sox lost 18 of their next 19 World Series and playoff games. The streak started with Game 6, which ended with the infamous error by Bill Buckner, and the Red Sox lost the Series two days later by dropping Game 7. Boston then was swept in their next three appearances in the playoffs, four games sweeps by Oakland in both the 1988 and 1990 ALCS and a three game sweep by Cleveland in the 1995 AL Division Series. In the 1998 Division

Series, Boston matched up against Cleveland again and won Game 1 at Jacobs Field but then dropped three in a row to the Indians. In the 1999 AL Division Series, Boston seemed destined to be swept again after losing the first two games to the Indians, but the Red Sox rallied to win three in a row to advance to the ALCS, where they lost to New York in five games.

Baltimore pitching great Jim Palmer won World Series games in three different decades. At age 20, Palmer won Game 2 of the 1966 World Series when he threw a four-hit, six-strikeout performance against Sandy Koufax and the Dodgers and won 6-0. In Game 1 of the 1970 Fall Classic, he went 8.2 innings, allowing three runs, and was the winner against the Cincinnati Reds. Palmer's next World Series win was in Game 2 in the 1971 World Series when he pitched eight strong innings and struck out ten Pirates. Palmer picked up his last World Series win – *and last career win* – in Game 3 of the 1983 World Series on October 14, the day before his 38th birthday. In his only appearance in the Series, Palmer entered in the fifth with the Orioles down 2-0 and worked two innings of scoreless relief and was the pitcher of record when his teammates rallied with one run in the sixth and two more in the seventh for a 3-2 win. Palmer retired in 1984 after starting the season 0-3 with a 9.17 ERA in five games.

The 1972 World Series between the Oakland A's and Cincinnati Reds featured a World Series record six games decided by one run, including three Oakland wins by the same score. The A's took the first two games in Cincinnati by scores of 3-2 and 2-1. Back in Oakland the Reds won the third game 1-0, but the A's came back to win the next one 3-2. The Reds forced the Series back to Cincinnati by winning Game 5 by a 5-4 score and evened the Series with the only blowout, a 8-1 win in Game 6. With the Series down to the deciding game, Oakland beat the Reds by a 3-2 score for the third time in seven games. As an indication of how close the Series was, each team collected 46 hits in 220 at-bats, an average of just .209.

Although he played from 1905 to 1928, won 12 batting titles, and set numerous offensive records, Ty Cobb never played on a World

Series winner. Cobb's Tigers lost three consecutive World Series from 1907 to 1909. The Tigers lost both the 1907 and 1908 World Series to the Chicago Cubs – who have not won a World Series since – and dropped the 1909 World Series to Pittsburgh. The only other franchise to lose three straight World Series is the New York Giants who lost three in a row from 1911 to 1913.

When the 1981 season resumed in August following the player's strike that began in June, the team that was in first place in each division when the strike began was declared the first half "winner" and, therefore, would participate in the playoffs along with the "winner" of second half of the season. This format kept the Cincinnati Reds and the St. Louis Cardinals out of the NL playoffs – *even though they had the two best records in the National League.* The Reds were a combined 66-42, better than any other team in *either league*, but they were 1/2 game back of Los Angeles when the strike hit and ended up 1 1/2 games back of Houston in the second half standings. The Cardinals finished 59-43 overall, but were second to Philadelphia by 1 1/2 games in the first half and trailed Montreal by 1/2 game in the second half.

Paul Molitor is the only player to get five hits in a World Series game. In Game 1 of the 1982 Series, Molitor collected five singles and drove in two runs for the Milwaukee Brewers as they beat the St. Louis Cardinals 10-0 at Busch Stadium.

The record for strikeouts in both an NLCS and ALCS game is 15 – *and they were set on successive days.* On October 11, 1997, Mike Mussina struck out 15 Indians in Game 3 of the ALCS in just seven innings but got a no-decision as Cleveland beat Baltimore 2-1 in 12 innings. The next day, Livan Hernandez fanned 15 to beat Greg Maddux and the Atlanta Braves 2-1 in Game 5 of the NLCS. In Game 4 of the 2000 ALCS, Roger Clemens tied Mussina's mark when he whiffed 15 Mariners.

The Texas Rangers have qualified for the playoffs just three times in their history – *and each time they lost in the Division Series to the eventual World Series champion New York Yankees.* In the first playoff game in Rangers' history in 1996, Texas beat New York 6-2 at Yankee Stadium. The Yankees responded by sweeping the next three in 1996, followed by three-game sweeps in 1998 and 1999. In the six games of the 1998 and 1999 Division Series, the Yankees outscored the Rangers by a combined total of 23 to 2.

Darold Knowles is the only pitcher to pitch in every game of a seven-game World Series. Oakland used Knowles in relief in each game as they beat the New York Mets in the 1973 World Series. He picked up saves in Games 1 and 7 and worked a total of 6.1 innings, giving up four hits and an unearned run while striking out five and walking five. Although he was also with Oakland when they won the AL pennant in 1972 and 1974, Knowles' only World Series appearances were the seven games in 1973.

Seven of the St. Louis Cardinals' nine World Series titles were won in seven games. Their first three World Series triumphs all went the distance – 1926, 1931 and 1934. Between 1946 and 1987, the St. Louis Cardinals played in seven World Series and each went the full seven games. They won four times (1946, 1964, 1967 and 1982) and lost three times (1968, 1985 and 1987).

Yogi Berra and Jose Canseco are the only two players to hit a grand slam in a World Series game that their team lost. Berra connected against Brooklyn's Don Newcombe in the second inning of Game 2 in 1956, but the Dodgers rallied to win 13-8. Canseco accounted for all four Oakland runs in their 5-4 loss to Los Angeles in Game 1 of the 1988 World Series when he homered against Tim Belcher in the second inning.

Johnny Mize played from 1936 to 1948 (missing 1943-1945 to World War II) without ever appearing in the World Series. Near the end of the 1949 season, he was traded to the New York Yankees and played in the Yankees' World Series victory over the Dodgers. He then finished his career with four more championships in his last four years as New York won each year from 1950 to 1953.

Boston's Marty Barrett tied a World Series record in 1986 when he collected 13 hits (to go with five walks) – *but he only managed to score one run.* Barrett hit in all seven games but did not cross the plate until the seventh inning of Game 6 when he walked and later scored on a ground out by Dwight Evans. Barrett entered the last game with 12 hits, needing two more to set a World Series record. He managed a bunt single in the second inning but then went 0 for 3, including a swinging strikeout to end Boston's 8-5 loss in Game 7. Barrett's great performance was wasted as Bill Buckner hit just .188 (6 for 32) batting behind him. Ironically, in the 1986 ALCS the week before, Barrett's teammate Jim Rice hit just .161 (5 for 31) with one walk yet scored *eight* times.

Pee Wee Reese is the only player to appear in all 44 World Series games played between the Brooklyn Dodgers and New York Yankees. Reese totaled 46 hits in 169 at-bats for a .272 average while scoring 20 runs, hitting three doubles, two triples, two homers and driving in 16 runs.

Jim Mason and Geoff Blum are the only players to hit a home run in their only World Series at-bat. Mason entered in the fifth inning of Game 3 of the 1976 World Series as a defensive replacement for the New York Yankees. He batted in the seventh inning and hit the only Yankee homer of the Series – and the 500th in World Series history – against Cincinnati's Pat Zachry before being removed for a pinch hitter in the ninth inning of the Yankees' 6-2 loss to the Reds. Blum entered Game 3 of the 2005 World Series as a defensive substitution in the 13th and lined a solo shot to right field an inning later against Houston reliever Ezequiel Astacio. Blum's 14th-inning homer, the latest in Series history, broke a 5-5 tie and propelled Chicago to a 7-5 win in the longest World Series game in history (five hours and 41 minutes).

There has been only one World Series in which the two teams scored *exactly* the same number of runs. Cleveland beat the Boston Braves in a six-game 1948 World Series in which each teams scored 17 runs.

Pittsburgh has a perfect record of 5-0 in Game 7s that decided the World Series. The Pirates won all five of their World Series championships (1909, 1925, 1960, 1971, and 1979), by winning the decisive seventh game of the Series. Pittsburgh did lose the seventh game of the 1903 World Series to Boston, but it was a best-of-nine format at that time.

Five players have racked up at least ten RBIs in a single World Series – *and the last four of them played on teams that lost the Series*. The first player to do it was Yogi Berra who had ten RBIs to lead New York to a seven-game victory over Brooklyn in 1956. Ted Kluszewski drove in ten for the 1959 White Sox, but Chicago lost in six games to the Los Angeles Dodgers. In the 1960 World Series, Bobby Richardson drove in 12 runs – still a World Series record – and teammate Mickey Mantle added 11 more, but the Pirates shocked the Yankees in seven games. Cleveland's Sandy Alomar, Jr. had ten RBIs in the 1997 World Series, but the Florida Marlins prevailed in seven games.

Despite 660 lifetime regular season home runs and playing in four World Series, Willie Mays never homered in the Fall Classic. Mays managed only 14 singles and three doubles in 71 World Series at-bats.

Although his 81 regular season home runs are the fewest of the 16 players with at least six World Series homers, Lenny Dykstra was the quickest player to reach the half-dozen mark. In just 50 at-bats in 13 World Series games, Dykstra homered twice for the New York Mets in 1986 against Boston and then four times for Philadelphia in 1993 against Toronto. The next fastest was Goose Goslin who needed 52 World Series at-bats to get to six homers but then hit just one more in his next batted 77 at-bats. Hank Bauer took the opposite approach of Dykstra – he batted 111 times in the World Series before hitting a homer but then connected for seven long balls in his final 77 at-bats.

The two closest sweeps in World Series history ended with the wining team outscoring the losing team by just six runs. In 1950 the

New York Yankees swept Philadelphia while outscoring them just 11-5, winning by scores of 1-0, 2-1 (ten innings), 3-2, and 5-2. Despite never leading by more than two runs *at any point* in the 2005 World Series, the Chicago White Sox took four straight from Houston by scores of 5-3, 7-6, 7-5 (14 innings), and 1-0.

From 1954 to 1958, the 40-home run plateau was reached 21 times and each World Series champion featured a 40-homer player. By contrast, from 1972 to 2003 a total of 66 players combined for 143 seasons of at least 40 home runs, but just two led their team to a World Series title – Mike Schmidt, who hit 48 for the 1980 Phillies, and Luis Gonzalez, who hit 57 for the 2001 Diamondbacks. From 1981 to 2000, the span between Schmidt and Gonzalez, the 40-homer mark was topped 98 times by 49 different players *but none won a championship*. When Boston ended their 86-year World Series drought in 2004 with a four-game sweep of St. Louis, they became the first champion since the 1961 New York Yankees to feature two players with 40 homers – Manny Ramirez (43) and David Ortiz (41).

In the 2004 American League Championship Series, the New York Yankees became the only team to lose a series after taking a 3-0 lead – *even though they set an ALCS record by scoring 45 runs*. Due to their big 19-8 win in Game 3, New York outscored Boston 45-41 despite losing four games to three.

Goose Goslin and Edgar Renteria are the only players to end a World Series both with a hit and by making an out. Goslin ended Game 7 of Washington's 1925 World Series loss to Pittsburgh by striking out looking against Red Oldham. Ten years later, he singled to right in the ninth inning to win Game 6 and the Series for the Tigers against the Cubs. Renteria's 11th-inning single for Florida in Game 7 of the 1997 World Series against Cleveland clinched the Marlins' first championship. In 2004 he was with St. Louis and ended Boston's sweep of the Cardinals by grounding back to pitcher Keith Foulke.

Curt Schilling's three World Series wins – Game 5 in 1993 with the Phillies, Game 1 in 2001 with the Diamondbacks and Game 2 in 2004 with the Red Sox – make him the only pitcher to win World Series games with three different clubs. In the 1993 National League Championship Series, Schilling was voted the Most Valuable Player – *despite not winning a game.* He made two starts against Atlanta, allowing only three earned runs in 16 innings and striking out 19 batters. Mitch Williams got the win in each of Schilling's starts as Philadelphia won each game in ten innings by the score of 4-3.

Chipper Jones collected six hits in 21 at-bats, including three doubles, and scored three runs in both the 1995 and 1996 World Series.

Scott Podsednik ended Game 2 of the 2005 World Series with a one-out home run in the bottom of the ninth against Houston closer Brad Lidge – *after not hitting a home run in 507 regular season at-bats in 2005.* Podsednik's unexpected blast made him the only player to bat more than 500 times in the regular season without a homer and then hit one in the World Series. Podsednik also homered in Game 1 of the 2005 ALDS against Boston to make him only the second player to do it in the playoffs, joining Lance Johnson who homered in Game 4 of the 1993 ALCS against Toronto after not connecting in 540 at-bats during the 1993 season.

The Florida Marlins had just two winning seasons in their first 11 years (1993-2003) – but won the World Series *both* of those seasons (1997 and 2003). In each of their championship seasons the Marlins were the National League wild card team, so despite winning two World Series, Florida has yet to win a *division* championship. The Marlins' next best record during their first 11 seasons was in 1996 when they finished 80-82. Florida had their third winning season in 2004 when they finished 83–79 but did not qualify for the playoffs.

With New York's Bill Bevens just one out away from a World Series no-hitter in 1947, Cookie Lavagetto's hit a pinch-hit double to right to score Al Gionfriddo and Eddie Miksis (pinch runners for Carl Furillo and Pete Reiser who had each walked) and make the Dodgers a 3-2 winner. The victory tied the Series at two games each, but the Yankees went on to beat Brooklyn in seven games. Bevens would pitch 2.2 innings of scoreless relief in Game 7, and then would never pitch in the majors again. The pinch-hit double was also Lavagetto's last career hit, as he was 0-4 for the rest of the Series and never played another game, finishing his career with 945 regular season hits. Another hero of the 1947 World Series was Al Gionfriddo who saved Game 6 for Brooklyn with a catch against the left field bullpen to rob Joe DiMaggio of a three-run, game-tying homer in the sixth inning. He never appeared in another major league game following his memorable grab.

From 2000 to 2003, the Oakland A's made the playoffs each season but lost in the American League Division Series, each time in five games – including *nine games* that would have advanced them to the ALCS. Tied at two games each in the 2000 ALDS against the Yankees, the A's lost the deciding fifth game. The next season they won the first two games against New York, only to drop the next three to lose the Series. The 2002 A's took two of the first three against the Twins but lost the last two to lose their third straight ALDS. Oakland's last appearance in the playoffs was in 2003 when they jumped to a quick two-game lead over the Red Sox in the ALDS, only to see Boston rally for three straight wins. Of Oakland's nine losses, four were decided by a single run and three others decided by two runs.

The Atlanta Braves had seven consecutive World Series losses that were decided by a *single run*. Atlanta lost a seven-game World Series the Minnesota Twins in 1991 with the final three losses coming by scores of 3-2, 4-3 (11 innings) and 1-0 (ten innings). The next season Toronto beat them in six games, winning by scores of 5-4, 3-2, 2-1 and 4-3 (11 innings). The Braves returned to the World Series in 1995 and beat the Indians in six games with their two losses coming by scores of 7-6 (11 innings) and 5-4. They also lost 8-6 in Game 4 of the 1996 World Series and 6-5 in Game 3 of the 1999 World Series, both times in ten innings, to make their record in extra-inning World Series games 0-6.

Sandy Alomar, Jr. (1997), Barry Bonds (2002) and David Ortiz (2004) are the only players to homer in the All-Star Game, Division Series, League Championship Series and World Series in the same season.

Willie Aikens is the only player to hit two homers in a game twice in the same World Series. In Game 1 of the 1980 World Series, Kansas City's Aikens cranked a two-run homer off Philadelphia's Bob Walk in the third inning and again in the eighth, but the Phillies still won 7-6. In Kansas City for Game 4, Aikens led Kansas City to a 5-3 win by walloped two more round-trippers, a two-run bomb in the first inning against Larry Christenson and a solo shot in the second off Dickie Noles.

The Oakland A's own the longest playoff or World Series winning streak by one team against another team by winning ten consecutive times against Boston. In 1988 and 1990, they swept the Red Sox in the ALCS and then won the first two of the 2003 ALDS before Boston rallied to win the next three. During their ten-game streak against Boston, they held the Sox to exactly one run seven times, including five consecutive games – the final game of the 1988 ALCS and all four games of the 1990 ALCS.

Matt Williams is the only player to hit a World Series home run for three different teams. Williams' first World Series homer was with San Francisco in the 1989 Series when he connected against Oakland's Dave Stewart in Game 3. Eight years later with Cleveland, Williams homered in Game 4 off Jay Powell of Florida and four years after that he went deep for Arizona in Game 2 of the 2001 Fall Classic against Yankees' pitcher Andy Pettitte. All three homers came in his home ballpark.

In his first 48 regular season starts, Josh Beckett did not have a single complete-game shutout – but then threw one in both the NLCS and the World Series to lead Florida to the title in 2003. With Chicago holding a 3-1 lead in the NLCS, one win away from their first World Series appearance since 1945, Beckett started the Marlins' comeback with a 4-0 win in Game 5 by hurling a two-hit,

11-strikeout masterpiece. He came out of the bullpen to pitch four innings of one-hit, one-run relief in Game 7 to help Florida hang on and take the NL pennant. Beckett started and lost Game 3 of the World Series to the New York Yankees despite fanning ten and allowing just three hits and two earned runs in 7.1 innings. In Game 6, Beckett took the mound at Yankee Stadium and wrapped up the title by overpowered New York, holding them to five hits and whiffing nine while winning 2-0.

The Houston Astros were the home team in the longest Division Series game, the longest Championship Series game and one of the two longest World Series games. The Astros lost Game 6 of the 1986 NLCS to the New York Mets in 16 innings by a 7-6 score. In 2005 they were involved in two classics, beating Atlanta 7-6 in Game 4 of the NLDS when Chris Burke homered in the bottom of 18th inning and losing to the Chicago White Sox in Game 3 of the World Series by a 7-5 score in 14 innings. Their Game 3 World Series loss tied the length of Game 2 of the 1916 Series between the Red Sox and Dodgers.

Aaron Small was 10-0 for the Yankees in the 2005 regular season but lost Game 3 of the ALDS, making him the only pitcher with a perfect regular season record of 5-0 or better to lose in the playoffs or World Series. Small relieved starter Randy Johnson in the top of the fourth of Game 3 with New York trailing the Angels 5-0. The Yankees rallied with four runs in the bottom of the fourth and then took the lead when they plated two more in the bottom of the fifth, but Small could not hold the Angels and gave up two runs before being taken out with two outs in the top of the sixth. The Angels went on to win 11-7 and make him the losing pitcher.

In Houston's classic 18-inning win against Atlanta in Game 4 of the 2005 NLDS, 43-year-old Roger Clemens entered in the bottom of the 15th for his first relief appearance since July 18, 1984. The first batter he faced was 47-year-old Julio Franco – *who he also faced in his first career game on May 15, 1984.* Clemens, the Astros last available pitcher and working on two days rest, threw three scoreless innings and got the win when Chris Burke homered in the bottom of the 18th. His victory made him the oldest pitcher to win either a playoff or World Series game.

The New York Yankees outscored the Pittsburgh Pirates 55 to 27 in the 1960 World Series – *yet lost the Series four games to three.* Pittsburgh won Games 1, 4, 5, and 7 by a total of seven runs while the Yankees took Games 2, 3, and 6 by a total margin of 35 runs. The Series concluded with Pittsburgh's dramatic 10-9 win over New York in Game 7 that ended with Bill Mazeroski's famous home run over the left field wall at Forbes Field. None of the five Yankees pitchers or the four Pirate hurlers recorded a strikeout in Game 7 – making it the *only* World Series game in which no batter struck out.

Clyde McCullough played in a World Series game in a year in which he did not appear in a regular season game. After returning from a two-year stint in the Navy, he rejoined the Cubs for the 1945 World Series against the Tigers. In his first at-bat since the 1943 season, McCullough pinch-hit against Hal Newhouser in the bottom of the ninth of the Cubs' Game 7 loss and struck out.

There were 54 strikeouts in the 1982 World Series between Milwaukee and St. Louis – *but no pitcher fanned more than three batters in a game.* Nine different pitchers tied for the lead with a three-strikeout game – Mike Caldwell in Games 1 and 5; Don Sutton, John Stuper, and Doug Bair in Game 2; Joaquin Andujar in Game 3; Dave LaPoint and Moose Haas in Game 4; Bob Forsch in Game 5; and Pete Vuckovich in Game 7.

About the Author

Madison McEntire is a 38-year-old structural engineer who, despite growing up in a small Arkansas town without a team, has been a lifelong baseball fan who enjoys reading about the game and its great history. He spends his summers playing and umpiring men's softball as well as helping coach his kids' teams. Madison has been a member of the Society for American Baseball Research (SABR) since 1992 and currently serves as the chairman of the Brooks Robinson – George Kell regional SABR chapter in Arkansas. He had an article published in SABR's *National Pastime* in 1996 and contributed baseball trivia lists that appeared in *Inside Sports* in the fall of 1997. In the winter of 2004, he contributed two baseball trivia tidbits that were included in the *Useless Information* columns of ESPN.com baseball writer Jayson Stark. Madison lives in Bryant, Arkansas, with his wife, Crissy, his two children, Mackenzie and Will, and their dog Wrigley. This is his first book.